Classroom English@TEE
TEE인증 대비 교실영어

Classroom English@TEE
TEE인증 대비 교실영어

이성희 · Heidi Nam 지음

한국문화사

Classroom English@TEE

초판인쇄 2012년 11월 20일
초판발행 2012년 11월 30일

지은이 이 성 희 · Heidi Nam
꾸민이 공 정 선
펴낸이 김 진 수
펴낸곳 **한국문화사**
등 록 1991년 11월 9일 제2-1276호
주 소 서울특별시 성동구 아차산로 3(성수동1가) 502호
전 화 (02)464-7708/3409-4488
전 송 (02)499-0846
이메일 hkm7708@hanmail.net
홈페이지 www.hankookmunhwasa.co.kr

책값은 뒤표지에 있습니다.

잘못된 책은 바꾸어 드립니다.
이 책의 내용은 저작권법에 따라 보호받고 있습니다.

ISBN 978-89-5726-236-8 13740

이 도서의 국립중앙도서관 출판시도서목록(CIP)은 e-CIP 홈페이지
(http://www.nl.go.kr/cip.php)에서 이용하실 수 있습니다.
(CIP제어번호: CIP2012005063)

| 머리말 |

    *Classroom English@TEE*는 영어로 진행하는 영어수업(Teaching English in English: TEE)을 실시하거나 영어수업능력 인증(TEE인증)을 받고자 하는 현직 영어 교사 및 예비 영어 교사들을 위하여 저술되었다. 따라서 이 책은 교육대학 및 사범대학 영어교육과의 TEE 관련 강의나 현직 영어 교사의 TEE 관련 재교육 강의의 교재로 사용되면 좋을 것이다. 더불어 이 책은 교생실습생 및 초·중등교원 임용고사 준비생, 그리고 교실영어(classroom English)를 독학으로 학습하고자 하는 교사에게도 요긴한 참고도서가 될 것이다. 이 책은 특히 영어가 모국어가 아닌 교사나 최근의 영어 교사 훈련을 체계적으로 받은 경험이 부족한 교사에게 좀 더 많은 도움이 될 것으로 본다.

*Classroom English@TEE*의 특징

    이 책의 특징은 다음과 같이 크게 여섯 가지로 나누어 볼 수 있다. (1) 이 책은 수년간의 교실 검증(classroom-tested)을 거쳐서 저술된 책이다. 이 책의 내용은 저자들이 가르치고 있는 대학의 영어교육과 TEE 관련 강의에서 교재로 채택되어 교사 훈련 과정에 적합하도록 그 내용과 구성이 수년간에 걸쳐 수정·보완된 것이다. 또한 현재 영어로 수업을 진행하고 있는 초등학교, 중학교 및 고등학교 현직 교사들의 의견 수렴을 거쳐 저술된 책이다. (2) 이 책은 우리 나라 국가수준 영어과 교육 과정에 포함된 의사소통 예시문과 동일한 표현들을 다수 포함하고 있고, 초등 및 중등 영어교과서의 교사용지도서에 포함된 교실영어를 선별하여 포함함으로써 국가 수준 영어과 교육과정이 제안하는 영어수업에 도움을 주고자 하였다. (3) 이 책은 국가영어능력평가시험(National English Ability Test: NEAT)에 대비하기 위한 말하기 활동(speaking activities)을 진행하는 데 필요한 표현들을 포함함으로써, NEAT에 좀 더 효과적으로 대비할 수 있도록 배려하였다. (4) 이 책은 교실영어를 선별하고 구성함에 있어서 그 기준을 교사와 학생, 그리고 학생과 학생간의 바람직한 언어 사용에 두었다. 즉 다툼, 분노, 불평, 저주 등에 사용되는 거친 표현들을 될수록 지양하고, 정직, 협동, 배려, 축복 등에 사용되는 알아듣기 쉬운 표현들을 포함하고자 노력하였다. (5) 이 책은 영어로 진행하는 영어수업에 익숙하지 않은 교사를 위하여 각 절마다 예시 대화문이나 핵심 예시문을 제시하고 있고, 영어교수법에 근거한 교실영어 사용 시의 도움말, 유의사항, 혹은 오용사례를 필요한 곳마다 삽입하여 교실영어를 쉽게 이해하고 사용할 수 있도록 하였다. 또한 필요할 때마다 교실영어 사용 맥락에 대한 간단한 설명을 괄호 안에 기술하였다. (6) 부록에는 각 Part별 복습문제와 정답(Review Exercises and Answer Key)을 포함하여 교사 혹은 학습자 스스로가 각 Part에 대한 학습 성취도를 평가할 수 있도록 하였다. 더불어 부록에 소논문 "Making Classroom English Comprehensible" (교실영어 이해하기 쉽게 만들기)을 포함함으로써, 교실영어를 단순화하고 좀 더 이해하기 쉽게 만드는 실제적이고 구체적인 방법들을 제시하였다.

*Classroom English@TEE*의 구성

이 책은 모두 6개 단원으로 구성되어 있다. Part 1은 수업 시작, Part 2는 수업 전개, Part 3은 언어 연습, Part 4는 교재 사용, Part 5는 수업 강화, Part 6은 수업 종료 과정과 관련된 교실영어로 이루어져 있다. 각 단원의 제목으로 보아 알 수 있듯이 이 책의 전반적인 내용 전개는 실제 수업의 일반적인 진행 순서 및 단계를 따르고 있다. 각 소단원이 시작되는 부분에는 해당 수업 단계에 대한 이해를 돕기 위하여 예시 대화문

혹은 핵심 예시문을 제시하였다. 각 소단원에 포함된 교실영어 표현들은 유사한 의미를 지니거나 유사한 상황에 사용되는 것들끼리 군을 이루어 제시되어 있다. 수업에서 사용되는 학생 영어(Student English)는 교사 영어(Teacher English)와 분리하여 제시하지 않고 동일한 소단원 내에 함께 제시함으로써, 학생과 교사가 수업 상황 및 맥락에 어울리는 표현을 융통성 있게 선택하여 사용할 수 있도록 하였다. 학생 영어는 '°' 문자를 삽입하여 구분하였다. 영어교수법에 근거한 교실영어 사용 시의 도움말, 유의사항 혹은 오용 사례를 제시한 부분은 도움말 문자를 사용하여 표시하였고, 오용 사례로 제시된 문장 앞에는 '*' 문자를 삽입하여 틀린 표현임을 나타냈다.

  이 책의 기획으로부터 탈고 및 교실 검증, 그리고 출판에 이르기까지 크고 작은 어려움에 봉착할 때마다 저자들에게 피할 곳을 예비해주시고, 때에 따라 필요한 지혜를 공급해주시며, 선한 길로 인도해주신 하나님께 무한한 감사를 드린다. 그리고 이 책의 내용이 교실 검증을 거치는 동안 진솔한 비판 및 제언을 아낌없이 개진해준 총신대학교 영어교육과 학생들에게 깊은 감사와 사랑의 마음을 전한다. 무엇보다도 이 책이 한정된 강의의 교재에서 벗어나 영어로 영어수업을 진행하거나 TEE 인증을 받고자 하는 더 많은 독자들에게 쉽게 읽혀질 수 있도록 적극적으로 도와주신 한국문화사 이진수 사장님께 깊은 감사의 말씀을 전하는 바이다.

2012년 10월
집필진 씀

| 차례 |

머리말 ··· v
차례 ··· ix

PART I The Beginning of the Lesson 수업 시작

1. Asking Students to Come In
   학생들이 교실로 들어오도록 요청하기 ································ 3
2. Greetings 인사하기 ··· 5
3. Introducing Yourself 자기 소개하기 ································· 8
4. Introducing Guests and New Students
   손님/새로 온 학생 소개하기 ··· 15
5. Using English Names 영어 이름 사용하기 ······················· 17
6. Checking Attendance 출석 점검하기: 지각, 결석, 질병 ········· 19
7. Making Up Missed Work 빠진 수업 내용 보충하기 ············ 31
8. Small Talk 수업 전 사소한 이야기하기 ···························· 33
9. Responding 응답하기 ·· 37
10. Date 날짜에 대하여 이야기하기 ······································ 39
11. Time 시간에 대하여 이야기하기 ······································ 41
12. Weather 날씨에 대하여 이야기하기 ·································· 42
13. Compliments 칭찬하기 ·· 43
14. Class Climate 교실 환경에 대하여 이야기하기 ··················· 45
15. Checking Homework 숙제 점검하기 ······························· 50
16. Review of the Previous Lesson 이전 수업 내용 복습하기 ······· 53

17. Transition to New Work 새로운 수업 내용으로 이동하기 ········· 56
18. Seating Arrangements 자리 정리하기 ································ 58
19. Getting Out School Supplies 수업 자료 꺼내기 ················ 60
20. Distribution of New Materials 새로운 수업 자료 배부하기 ······· 64

PART II The Development of the Lesson 수업 전개

1. Introducing the Subject/Course 과목/강의 소개하기 ············ 73
2. Introducing Today's Lesson 오늘의 수업 소개하기 ············ 78
3. Sequencing 수업 내용의 순서 정하기 ······························· 79
4. Moving On 수업 진도 나가기 ··· 82
5. Taking a Break 휴식 시간 갖기 ·· 84
6. Starting Again/Back to Work 수업 다시 시작하기 ············· 85
7. Using Korean/English 한국어/영어 사용하기 ···················· 86
8. Student Presentation 학생 발표하기 ································· 88
9. Repetition and Responses 반복 및 응답하기 ···················· 89
10. Choral Response 전체 및 응답하기 ································· 90
11. Individual Response 개인 응답하기 ································· 92
12. Taking Turns 순서 교체하기 ·· 93
13. Class in Halves 분반하기 ··· 97
14. Individual Work 개인 활동하기 ·· 99
15. Pairwork 짝 활동하기 ··· 100
16. Group Work 그룹 활동하기 ·· 103
17. Dividing into Teams 팀 나누기 ······································· 108
18. Asking for Volunteers 자원자 요청하기 ·························· 110
19. Movement, General Activity 동작, 일반 활동하기 ··········· 112
20. Leaving the Classroom 교실 나가기 ······························· 118
21. Checking Comprehension 이해력 점검하기 ···················· 119
22. Asking for Clarification 설명 요청하기 ··························· 123
23. Giving Feedback 피드백 제공하기 ·································· 125

24. Confirmation 확인하기 ··· 126
25. Leading to the Answer 정답 유도하기 ···························· 131
26. Encouragement 격려하기 ·· 133
27. Evaluation 평가하기 ·· 135
28. Giving Opinions 의견 제시하기 ······································· 137
29. Showing Preference 선호하는 것 제시하기 ···················· 141
30. Explaining and Giving Examples 설명 및 예시하기 ············ 144
31. Class Control and Discipline 수업 통제하기 및 훈육하기 ············ 146
32. Establishing Rules 규칙 설정하기 ···································· 147
33. Getting Attention 주의 집중시키기 ·································· 150
34. Warning 경고하기 ·· 152
35. Giving Permission 허락하기 ··· 155
36. Apologizing 사과하기 ·· 158
37. Offering Help 도움주기 ··· 160
38. Thanking 감사하기 ·· 161
39. Giving 나누기 ·· 163
40. Congratulating/Well Wishing 축하/축복하기 ··················· 165

PART III   Language Practice 언어 연습

1. Spelling 철자법에 대하여 이야기하기 ······························ 169
2. Pronunciation 발음에 대하여 이야기하기 ························ 174
3. Vocabulary 단어에 대하여 이야기하기 ···························· 178
4. Grammar 문법에 대하여 이야기하기 ······························· 182
5. Listening 듣기 ··· 187
6. Storytelling 이야기 말하기 ·· 192
7. Asking for Clarity and Volume 명확성 및 소리 크기 요청하기 ······ 194
8. Brainstorming 브레인스토밍하기 ······································ 195
9. Dialogue 대화하기 ·· 196
10. Show and Tell 보여주며 말하기 ······································ 201

11. Acting Out/Skit 연극/촌극하기 ······················· 204
12. Discussion 토론하기 ····················· 208
13. Reading 읽기 ······················· 215
14. Writing 쓰기 ······················· 221
15. Handwriting 손으로 쓰기 ····················· 225
16. Doing Exercises 연습활동하기 ··················· 227
17. Games 게임하기 ····················· 233
18. Songs and Chants 노래와 챈트하기 ················ 242
19. Drawing 그림 그리기 ··················· 247

PART IV Using Teaching Aids and Electrical Equipment
교구 및 기자재 사용

1. Textbook 교과서 사용하기 ····················· 253
2. Locating Pages 페이지 찾기 ···················· 254
3. Locating Things on the Page 페이지에서 원하는 것 찾기 ············ 256
4. Blackboard/White Board/Magnet Board
   칠판/백판/자석판 사용하기 ····················· 260
5. Word Cards 단어카드 사용하기 ··················· 265
6. Picture Cards/Pictures 그림카드/사진 사용하기 ············· 268
7. Work Cards/Worksheets 워크카드/워크시트 사용하기 ·········· 271
8. Information Gaps 정보차 활동하기 ················· 274
9. Flannel Board 융판 사용하기 ··················· 275
10. Wall Pictures/Wall Posters 벽 그림/벽 포스터 사용하기 ········· 276
11. Newspapers/Publicity Materials 신문/광고자료 사용하기 ········ 277
12. Graphs, Charts, Maps 그래프, 도표, 지도 사용하기 ·········· 280
13. Finger Puppets 손가락 인형 사용하기 ················ 282
14. Audio/Video Recordings 오디오 녹음/비디오 녹화 자료 사용하기 ··· 285
15. Videotaping 녹화하기 ····················· 290
16. Beam Projector/PPT 빔 프로젝터/PPT 기기 사용하기 ·········· 291

17. Language Lab 어학실습실 사용하기 ·· 293
18. Computers 컴퓨터 사용하기 ·· 295
19. Problematic Equipment 기자재 문제/고장에 대하여 이야기하기 ······· 299

PART V   Consolidation of the Lesson 수업 강화

1. Review of the Lesson 복습하기 ·· 303
2. Testing: Exams and Quizzes 평가: 시험 및 퀴즈보기 ················· 306
3. NEAT Speaking Activities
   국가영어능력평가시험의 말하기 활동하기 ····································· 313
4. Giving Homework 숙제 부과하기 ··· 315

PART VI   The End of the Lesson 수업 종료

1. Almost Time to Stop 종료 시간이 다가옴을 알리기 ····················· 321
2. Stop Working 활동 종료하기 ·· 323
3. Preparation for the Next Class 다음 수업 준비하기 ···················· 324
4. Collecting Materials 교재 수거하기 ··· 326
5. Cleaning Up 정리하기 ·· 327
6. Ending the Lesson 수업 종료하기 ··· 329
7. Seasonal Greetings 절기 인사하기 ·· 330
8. Saying Goodbye 작별 인사하기 ··· 332

Appendix 1

Review Exercises and Answer Key 복습 문제 및 정답

Part 1   Review Exercises ·· 337
Part 2   Review Exercises ·· 341
Part 3   Review Exercises ·· 345
Part 4   Review Exercises ·· 348
Part 5   Review Exercises ·· 350
Part 6   Review Exercises ·· 352

Answer Key to Part 1 Review Exercises ··· 354
Answer Key to Part 2 Review Exercises ··· 357
Answer Key to Part 3 Review Exercises ··· 360
Answer Key to Part 4 Review Exercises ··· 362
Answer Key to Part 5 Review Exercises ··· 364
Answer Key to Part 6 Review Exercises ··· 366

Appendix 2
Making Classroom English Comprehensible
교실영어 이해하기 쉽게 만들기 ·· 371

찾아보기 ·· 377

PART I

The Beginning of the Lesson
수업 시작

PART I

The Beginning of the Lesson
수업 시작

1. Asking Students to Come In 학생들이 교실로 들어오도록 요청하기
2. Greetings 인사하기
3. Introducing Yourself 자기 소개하기
4. Introducing Guests and New Students 손님/새로 온 학생 소개하기
5. Using English Names 영어 이름 사용하기
6. Checking Attendance 출석 점검하기: 지각, 결석, 질병
7. Making Up Missed Work 빠진 수업 내용 보충하기
8. Small Talk 수업 전 사소한 이야기하기
9. Responding 응답하기
10. Date 날짜에 대하여 이야기하기
11. Time 시간에 대하여 이야기하기
12. Weather 날씨에 대하여 이야기하기
13. Compliments 칭찬하기
14. Class Climate 교실 환경에 대하여 이야기하기
15. Checking Homework 숙제 점검하기
16. Review of the Previous Lesson 이전 수업 내용 복습하기
17. Transition to New Work 새로운 수업 내용으로 이동하기
18. Seating Arrangements 자리 정리하기
19. Getting Out School Supplies 수업 자료 꺼내기
20. Distribution of New Materials 새로운 수업 자료 배부하기

1 Asking Students to Come In
학생들이 교실로 들어오도록 요청하기

Teacher: Hello, Jin-ho. Come in. Who's still out in the hallway?
Student: Min-ho.
Teacher: Could you ask him to come in?
Student: Okay. (학생이 복도로 나간다.) Min-ho, come in.

- Come in.
- Come in and sit down.
- Come in and have a seat.
- Come in and close the door.
- Come in and join us.

- Who's out in the hallway?
- Who's still out in the hallway?
- I hear some people in the hallway.
- I think there are still some people coming.
- Is anyone still out in the hallway?

- Please ask Min-ho to come in.
- Could/Would you ask your friends to come in?
- Myung-ja, could you tell everyone else to come in?
- Could you ask him to come in so we can get started?

◦ Min-ho.
◦ Min-ho is.

I. The Beginning of the Lesson

- Okay.
- Sure.
- All right.
- Yes, sir/ma'am.
- Yes, Mr. Lee.
- Yes, Mrs. Kim

> **도움말**
>
> 교사가 학생들이 다른 학생들에게 지시사항을 전달해달라고 요청할 때는 'Ask your friends to come in'에서와 같이 'ask (person) to (verb)' 혹은 'tell (person) to (verb)'라는 표현을 사용할 수 있습니다.
>   incorrect: *Ask to your friends to come in.
>   correct: Ask your friends to come in.

> **도움말**
>
> 학생들이 간혹 교사의 성별(gender)에 관계없이 항상 'Yes, sir.'이라고 답하는 경우가 있는데, 성별에 따라 sir와 ma'am을 잘 선별하여 사용해야 한다는 것을 알려줄 필요가 있습니다. Mr.외에도 Miss, Mrs., Ms. 등의 호칭을 교사의 성(last name)에 붙여 사용할 수 있습니다. Mr. Smith, Mrs. Jones, Ms. Lee 등이 그 예입니다. Ms.는 기혼이나 미혼 여성 모두에게 사용하며 [miz]라고 발음합니다. 학생들이 수업 중 교사를 부를 때 'teacher'라고 하거나 교사의 이름(first name)을 부르는 것은 교사가 그렇게 부르는 것을 허락한 경우가 아니면 실례가 될 수도 있습니다.

2 Greetings
인사하기

Teacher: Good morning, everyone.
Students: Good morning, Mr. Lee.
Teacher: It's good to see you again. Hello, Geum-ju.
How are you today?
Student: I'm okay, thanks.

- Hi.
- Hello.
- Good morning/afternoon/evening.
- Hello, everyone. Nice to see you.

○ Hi.
○ Hello, Mr. Lee.
○ Good morning, Mr. Lee.

도움말

위의 인사말들을 그대로 반복하여 상대방에게 다시 말하면 상대방을 향한 적절한 인사말이 됩니다. 첫 인사를 할 때는 상대방의 나이나 결혼 여부, 월급 등 매우 개인적인 내용을 묻지 않도록 주의해야 합니다. 그리고 한국 사람들의 일상적인 인사인 '식사하셨어요?', '어디 가세요?' 등의 질문은 특별한 목적을 가지고 묻는 경우를 제외하고는 묻지 않는 것이 일반적입니다. 여기에서 특별한 경우란 예를 들면 상대방과 함께 식사하러 가고자 하는 경우에 'Did you have lunch?'라고 상대방에게 묻는 경우입니다. 이 때 상대방이 허락한다면 함께 식사하러 갈 수도 있을 것입니다.

- How are you?
- How are you doing?
- How's everything?
- How are things?
- How's it going?
- How have you been?
- Long time, no see.
- What's up?

> **도움말**
> 위의 인사는 서로 알고 지내는 교사와 학생 사이나 혹은 학생과 학생 사이에 사용할 수 있습니다. 'How's it going?'과 'What's up?'은 격식을 차리지 않아도 되는 사이에 사용할 수 있는 표현입니다.

○ Fine, (thanks.)
○ I'm okay, thanks.
○ Pretty good.
○ Okay. How about you?
○ Not (too/so) good.
○ Not (too/so) bad, thanks.

> **도움말**
> 'How are you?'는 단순한 인사말이므로 상대방에게 'How are you?'라는 인사를 받았을 때 'I'm Fine. How about you?' 정도로 상대방에게 인사하면 됩니다. 상대방이 특별한 관심을 표하지 않는 한 자신이 어떻게 지내고 있는지에 대한 상세한 내용을 인사말에 반드시 포함할 필요는 없습니다.

- Welcome.
- It's good to see you.
- I'm glad you're all here.
- Thanks for coming.

3 Introducing Yourself
자기 소개하기

Teacher: My name is Ms. Park and I'll be teaching you English this year. First let me tell you a bit about myself. I grew up in Busan and then I moved to Seoul when I went to college. When I'm not teaching, I like playing with my dog and listening to music. Do any of you like listening to music, too? Most of you? Great! Do you want to know anything else about me? ... I hope we can get to know each other better and I hope you enjoy the class.

Student: Hi. My name is Jae-Young Lee. My English name is Mike. I like basketball and computer games. I like Starcraft best. I have a collection of Pokemon stickers. I have about 500 stickers. My favorite subject is English. I need to speak English well because I want to be a foreign service officer. I hope I can get to know you better.

- Nice to meet you.
- It's nice to meet you.
- I'm glad to meet you.
- It's a pleasure meeting you.
- I've been looking forward to meeting you.

> **도움말**
> 위의 인사는 학생과 교사가 처음 만나는 수업 시간에 사용할 수 있습니다. 같은 학생들과 다시 만나는 수업에서는 'Hi, everyone. It's nice to see you again.'이라고 인사할 수 있습니다.

- Let me introduce myself.
- Let me introduce myself to you.
- Let's start off with introductions.
- I'd like to tell a few things about myself.

- Would you introduce yourselves?
- I'd like you each to say something about yourselves.
- Now it's your turn. Tell me something about you.

> **도움말**
> '나를 소개하겠습니다.' 라고 말할 때는 아래와 같이 전치사 'to'를 포함합니다.
>   'Let me introduce myself to you.'

- Nice to meet you, too.
- Nice to meet you, Ms. Park.

- My name is Ms. Park.
- I'm Ji-young.
- My name's Ji-young.
- You can call me Mr. Lee.
- Please call me Ms. Cha.

I. The Beginning of the Lesson

- I'm your new English teacher.
- I'll be your English teacher this year.
- I'm going to teach you English this semester.
- I'm here to teach you English this year/semester/week.
- I'm a student teacher from A University.
- I'll be student teaching this month.
- I'm student teaching here until the end of May.

- I'm your substitute teacher today.
- I'm substitute teaching today for Mrs. Shin.
- Mrs. Shin is out of town, so I'll be with you today and tomorrow.
- Mrs. Shin couldn't be here today, so I'm filling in.

- If you want to meet me, you can come to the teacher's office.
- If you need to talk to me outside of class, you can find me in the teacher's office.
- When I'm not teaching, I'm usually in the teacher's office.

- The teacher's office is on the third floor of Building 3.
- Do you know where the teacher's office? It's on the third floor of Building 3.
- If you want to find the teacher's office, go to Building 3. It's on the third floor.

- My desk is on the right by the windows.
- My desk is the one next to the door.
- You can find my table in the back of the office.

- My e-mail address is ...
- You can e-mail me at ...
- If you need to reach me at home, you can call ...
- My phone number is...

- I'm from ...
- I grew up in Cheon-an.
- I come from Cheon-an originally.
- I grew up in Cheon-an until middle school.

- I moved to Seoul when I went to college.
- I came to Seoul last summer.
- I came to Seoul one year ago.
- I've been living here since last year.

- I live in ...
- I live just down the street.
- I live out of town, and it takes me forty minutes to get here everyday.

- I like basketball.
- I like playing baseball.
- I enjoy travelling a lot.

- Do you have any hobbies?
- What do you do for fun?
- What do you like to do in your spare time?
- What do you usually do after school?
- What do you like doing on Sundays?

- Do you have any other questions for me?
- Do you want to know anything else about me?
- Is there anything else you want to know about me?
- What else would you like to know?
- You can ask me questions.

> **도움말**
>
> 첫 수업일수록 교사의 질문에 대답하는 것에 대하여 부끄러워하거나 긴장하는 학생들이 있습니다. 이러한 경우에는 'Do you like computer games? stickers? sports?'와 같은 선택형 질문을 통하여 학생들이 쉽게 응답할 수 있도록 도와주는 것이 좋습니다. 또한 이러한 경우에는 교사가 개인 학생에게 질문을 하기 전에 아래와 같이 먼저 전체나 그룹에게 질문을 하는 것이 좋습니다.
>
> For example:
>
>   Teacher: Who likes computer games? Raise your hands. (초급 학생들인 경우에는 교사가 손을 들어 보여준다.) Good. Who likes collecting stickers? Now, Hee-Yong, what do you like to do in your spare time?

- I like computer games.
- I enjoy swimming.
- I collect stickers.
- I hang out with my friends.

> **도움말**
>
> 아래와 같이 선호하는 것을 표현할 때에는 복수형을 사용합니다.
>   incorrect: *I like computer game.
>   correct: I like computer games.

- What are you interested in?
- What's your favorite subject?
- Are you interested in Korean history?
- What kind of music do you like?

○ I like all kinds of music.
○ I especially like hip-hop.
○ I'm not interested in sports.
○ I don't have much interest in pop-music.

- What do you want to be when you grow up?
- What do you want to do when you get older?
- What's your dream job?

○ I want to be an astronaut.
○ I want to be a computer programmer.

- I hope we can get to know each other better.
- I'm looking forward to learning more about you.
- I'm sure we will learn more about each other this semester.

> **도움말**
>
> 'look forward to (something)'은 앞으로 일어날 일에 대한 긍정적인 느낌을 표현하는 말입니다. 그러나 'expect' 는 앞으로 일어날 일에 대하여 반드시 긍정적인 느낌만을 표현하는 것은 아니므로 그 차이를 알아둘 필요가 있습니다.

- I hope you enjoy the class.
- I hope you work hard and have fun this semester.
- I'm sure we will enjoy working together.

> **도움말**
>
> 이 상황에서는 'I wish' 라는 표현 보다는 'I hope' 라는 표현이 더 좋습니다. 'hope' 라는 표현을 사용 할 때는 가능성이 있거나 진심으로 바라는 경우에 사용되며, 'wish'는 가능성이 없는 일을 바라거나 사실이 아닌 경우에 사용합니다.
>
> 'work hard'는 최선을 다한다는 의미로 사용됩니다. 'work hardly'와 같이 부사형을 함께 사용하는 것은 올바른 표현이 아닙니다. 열심히 하지 않는다는 표현으로 'hardly work'를 사용할 수는 있습니다.

4. Introducing Guests and New Students
손님/새로 온 학생 소개하기

> Teacher: We have a visitor today. This is my friend Mr. Jeong.
> Can you all say 'Hello' to Mr. Jeong?
> Students: Hello.
> Teacher: He will be watching our class today.
> He wants to see a normal class, so just pretend he isn't there.

- This is your new classmate, Min-ho.
- This is my friend, Mr. Jeong.
- I'd like you to meet Min-ho.
- I'd like to introduce a new friend to you.

- We have a visitor today.
- We have several guests today.
- Mr. Jeong will be watching our class today.
- Mr. and Mrs. Hwang are going to tell us about their experiences in Australia.

- Let's welcome Mr. Jeong.
- Will you please give a warm welcome to Mr. Jeong.
- Can you all say 'Hello' to Mr. Jeong?
- Hello.

> **도움말**
> 'please give a warm welcome ...'이란 표현이 학생들에게 익숙하지 않은 경우에는 교사가 박수를 쳐서 이해를 도울 수 있습니다.

- Just act normal.
- Act like you always do.
- He wants to see a normal class, so just pretend he isn't there.

- Do you have any questions for Mrs. Shin?
- Is there anything you would like to ask Mrs. Shin?
- This is your chance to ask questions to Mrs. Shin.

5 Using English Names
영어 이름 사용하기

Teacher: I'd like you all to choose English names in this class. If you don't have an English name then you need to find one. Here is a list of English names. You can choose one of these names. Or if you want me to choose a name, you can say, 'Could you give me an English name?' Let me write that on the board. (교사가 칠판에 'Could you give me an English name?' 이라고 적는다.) Now when I call your Korean name, you give me your English name. You can say 'My name is ...' Sae-ri, do you have an English name?
Student: No.
Teacher: Not yet?
Student: Not yet. Could you give me an English name?
Teacher: How about Sally? Is that okay?

- You need an English name for this class.
- I'd like you all to choose English names in this class.
- Could each of you make an English name for this class?
- If you don't have an English name then you need to find one.

- Here is a list of English names.
- You can choose one of these names.
- You may use one of the names on this list.
- Look at this list and find a name.

- What's your English name?
- Do you have an English name?
  ◦ Yes. (I do.)/No. (I don't./Not yet.)
- Have you picked an English name?
  ◦ Yes. (I have.)/No. (I haven't./Not yet.)

> **도움말**
> 'not yet'이란 표현은 학습자들이 나중에 할 수도 있다는 여지를 두는 것으로 유용한 학생 영어의 한 표현입니다.

  ◦ I'm Brenden.
  ◦ My English name is Brenden.

  ◦ I don't have an English name.
  ◦ I want an English name.
  ◦ Could you give me an English name?
  ◦ I'd rather use my Korean name.

- Do you like the name 'Sally'?
- Is Sally all right?
- How about 'Sally'? Is that okay?

> **도움말**
> 'How about …' 이란 표현은 제안할 때 사용되는 표현으로서 대화를 시작하는 상황에서는 사용하지 않는 것이 좋습니다.

6 Checking Attendance
출석 점검하기: 지각, 결석, 질병

Teacher: I'm going to call the roll. When I call your name, please say 'here'. Young-min.
Young-min: Here.

- I'll take attendance now.
- I'm going to call the roll.
- Let me fill in the attendance chart.
- When I say your name, say, 'Here'.
- When you hear your name, say, 'Here'.
- Listen for your names as I call the roll.
- When I call your name, please respond by saying, 'Yes'.

도움말

교사가 학생의 이름을 부를 때 종종 학생은 우리말로 대답을 하게 됩니다. 이러한 경우에는 아래와 같이 교사가 영어 답변을 권유할 필요가 있습니다.

Teacher: Young-min.
Young-min: 네
Teacher: Here.
Young-min: Here.

- Is anyone absent?
- Is everyone here?
- Who is gone today?
- Who isn't here?

◦ Mi-sun is gone.
◦ Ji-myung is absent.

> **도움말**
>
> 교사는 학생들이 간단한 문장의 연습을 통하여 완전한 문장을 구사할 수 있도록 아래와 같이 도울 수 있습니다.
>
> Teacher: Who isn't here?
> Student: Mi-sun.
> Teacher: Oh, yes. Mi-sun is gone.

- Is there anyone who didn't hear their name?
- Is there anyone whose name I didn't call?
- Is there anyone else here who is not on the list?

◦ I'm here.
◦ Did you get me?
◦ You didn't call me/my name.

◦ Sorry. I just got here.
◦ I just came in when you said/called my name.

- You should pay attention.
- You should have been listening.
- Pay attention next time when I take the roll.

1 LATENESS 지각

> Teacher: Oh, Hee-jin. Did you just get here?
> Student: Yes.
> Teacher: Where were you? Did you oversleep?
> Student: Sorry. I missed the bus.
> Teacher: Well, try to be on time tomorrow.
> Student: Okay. I won't do it again.

- Eun-ju, you made it.
- Oh, Yong-jin just walked in.
- Did you just get here? Yes.

○ Sorry. I just got here.
○ I just came in now.
○ I just came in when you called my name.

(출석 점검 중)
- We've already passed your name.
- I have already marked you as 'absent'.
- Sorry, I called your name already.

- Why are you late?
- Why weren't you on time?
- Why weren't you here when class started?

- Where were you?
- Where have you been?
- What were you doing?
- What took you so long?

- Did you oversleep?
- Didn't your alarm go off?
- Did you wake up late this morning?
- Was there a traffic jam?
- Did you miss the bus?

> **도움말**
>
> 북미사람들은 종종 'Why are you late?'이라고 묻는 것은 정중한 표현이 아니라고 생각합니다. 이러한 경우에는 'Where were you?' 라고 묻는 것이 더 부드러운 표현이라고 할 수 있습니다.

○ Sorry I'm late.
○ Sorry, I didn't hear the bell.
○ I got up late, so I missed the bus.

- I have to mark you absent.
- You are too late. I can't give you credit for being here.
- If you want me to mark you 'here,' you have to come on time.

- You are 10 minutes late.
- Class started 10 minutes ago.
- You should have been here 10 minutes ago.

> **도움말**
>
> '10 minutes before'는 학생들이 자주 사용하는 틀린 표현입니다. '10 minutes ago'가 맞는 표현임을 학생들에게 알려줄 필요가 있습니다.
>
>   incorrect: *10 minutes before
>   correct: 10 minutes ago

- If you are late 3 times, it counts as an absence.
- 3 'lates' will affect your grade like 1 absence.
- Your first 'late' doesn't matter — but if you walk in late 3 times, I will treat them like an absence.

- Don't be late again.
- Try not to be late again.
- Try to be on time tomorrow.
- You should come to class by nine o'clock.
- For next time, remember: class starts at nine o'clock.
- You should really be here at the beginning of class.

○ Okay. I won't do it again.

2 ABSENCE 결석

> Teacher: Where's Hye-su? Did anyone talk to Hye-su today?
> Student: Yes.
> Teacher: Is she coming?
> Student: No, she had a doctor's appointment.
> Teacher: Ji-myung, can you help Hye-su when she comes back?

- I don't see Geum-ju today.
- Jun-sung's gone. Oh, that's too bad.
- It looks like Song-jin isn't here.

- Where's Hye-su?
- Does anyone know where Min-ju is?
- Did anyone talk to Han-jun today?
- Does anyone know why Hyun-sok is gone?

도움말

학생들은 영어로 대답해야 하는 것을 모르거나 영어로 어떻게 대답할지 몰라서 망설일 수 있습니다. 적절한 예시 문장을 학생들에게 제공하면 학생들이 다소 편하게 답할 수 있습니다.
'Is she sick? Is she gone?...' 혹은 'I haven't seen him.' 등이 그 예입니다.

- She's sick today.
- He had a doctor's appointment.
- He wasn't here this morning.
- No, I haven't seen him.

- Say Hello to Hye-su (for me).
- Tell Su-min I said, 'Hello.'
- If you see Hee-jin, tell her I said, 'Hi,' okay?

- Is she coming?
- Is she on her way?
- Do you know if she's planning to be here?

○ She's coming.
○ She'll be here in ten minutes.
○ She won't be here this week.
○ She'll probably come.
○ I doubt if she will.
○ I don't know.
○ I'm not sure.

> 도움말
>
> 'She'll be here after 10 minutes.'는 틀린 표현입니다. 'She'll be here in 10 minutes.'가 올바른 표현입니다.

- Who was absent last time?
- Who wasn't here on Monday?
- Someone was gone on Monday. Who was it?
- Mi-jin was absent/gone.

> **도움말**
>
> 아래와 같이 'absent'는 형용사로만 사용할 수 있고, 동사로는 사용할 수 없습니다.
>
>   incorrect: *She absented.
>   correct: She was absent.

- Jun-yeok, welcome back.
- Hyun-jin, it's nice to see you again.
- Han-na, we've missed you.

- We missed you yesterday.
- You were gone last time, right?
- You weren't here on Friday, were you?

  ○ Yes./No, I was here.

- We haven't seen you for a while.
- You haven't been here in a while.
- You've been out since Monday.
- How long have you been gone?
- I was gone Monday and Tuesday.
- I've been sick for two days.

- What happened?
- What was the matter?
- Why were you gone last time?
- Why weren't you here?
- Where were you?

- I was sick.
- (I was gone) because I was sick.
- I had to go to the doctor.
- I had driver's training.

> **도움말**
>
> 학생이 무엇인가 말하려고 할 때에 교사는 학생의 실수보다는 의사소통을 성공한 것에 대하여 관심을 가져주는 것이 좋습니다. 이 때 교사는 학생이 틀리게 말한 문장을 문법적으로 올바른 문장으로 바꾸어 말해줌으로써 학생의 이해를 도울 수 있습니다.
> For example:
>   Teacher: What happened?
>   Student: I must go doctor.
>   Teacher: Oh, you had to go to the doctor. Are you okay?

- So-ra, can you help Geum-ju when she comes back?
- So-ra, will you tell Geum-ju what we're doing today?
- So-ra, can you explain the homework to Geum-ju?

- Okay.

- If you miss more than four classes, then you will fail the course.
- If you are gone for more than four times, then I will have to fail you.
- If you have more than four absences, you'll automatically get an F.
- Don't miss more than four classes. If you do, you'll fail.

I. The Beginning of the Lesson

3 ILLNESS 질병

> Teacher: Did you catch a cold?
> Student: Yes.
> Teacher: How do you feel now?
> Student: I'm okay. Thanks.

- What's wrong?
- Are you sick?
- Don't you feel well?

◦ I'm okay.
◦ I have a headache.

- Were you sick?
- Did you catch a cold?
- Didn't you feel well?
- Were you a little under the weather?

도움말

'catch a cold'라는 표현은 종종 잘못 사용되고 있습니다. 감기에 걸린 것을 아는 순간 이미 감기가 시작된 것이 되므로 'caught a cold' (past tense) 혹은 'has a cold' (present tense) 로 표현하는 것이 맞습니다.

- Yes./Yes, I was.
- I had a cold.

- That's too bad.
- Oh, I'm sorry to hear that.
- That isn't much fun, is it?
- No, it isn't.

- How do you feel now?
- How are you feeling today?
- Are you feeling better now?
- Are you getting over it?
- I hope you're feeling better.

- I'm okay. Thanks.
- I'm a lot better now.
- I don't feel well.
- I'm still a little sick. Thanks for asking.

- Bless you! (재채기하는 사람에게 종종 사용하는 표현입니다.)

④ THE TEACHER'S ILLNESS 교사의 질병

> Teacher: Sorry. I'm not feeling very well today. I have a sore throat, so I can't talk any louder than this.

- I don't feel well.
- Sorry, I'm not feeling very well today.
- I'm a little under the weather.
- I think I'm coming down with the flu/a cold.

- I have a sore throat.
- I'm afraid I can't talk any louder.
- I think I'm losing my voice.

- I have a sore throat, so I can't talk any louder than this.
- Would you mind if I sit? I'm feeling a little sick.
- I don't feel well, so we'll stop class a little early today.

7 Making Up Missed Work
빠진 수업 내용 보충하기

Teacher: You were gone last time, weren't you?
Student 1: Yes.
Teacher: Well, you'll have to find out what we did. Why don't you talk to So-ra about the homework assignment? (So-ra에게) So-ra, could you tell Jin-won what we did yesterday?
Student 2: Okay.

- Ask a friend what we did last time.
- Why don't you talk to So-ra about the homework assignment.
- Maybe one of your classmates can tell you what we've done.

- Jin-ho, please tell Mi-ra what we did yesterday.
- Jin-ho, could you tell Mi-ra what we did yesterday?
  (공식적인 표현임)
- Mi-ra needs some help. Jin-ho, would you mind explaining what we did yesterday?

도움말

아래의 문장들은 전치사와 목적어를 어떻게 사용해야 하는지를 알려줍니다.
  talk to (person) about (topic)
  tell (person) about (topic)
  explain (topic) to (person)

I. The Beginning of the Lesson | 31

- This is the material we covered while you were gone.
- While you away, we practiced ...
- Last time we worked with ...

8 Small Talk
수업 전 사소한 이야기하기

> Teacher: Did you go anywhere over vacation?
> Student: Yes.
> Teacher: Where did you go?
> Student: Jeju Island.
> Teacher: Did you have fun?
> Student: Yeah.

- Did you have a good weekend?
- Did you enjoy the weekend?
- Did you have a nice summer/winter vacation?
- Did you do anything interesting over the weekend?

- Did you go anywhere over vacation?
- Did anyone go outside of Seoul?
- Raise your hand if you went somewhere over the holiday.

- What did you do?
- What is the most interesting thing you did?

◦ Jeju Island./I went to Jeju Island.

I. The Beginning of the Lesson

- Did you have a good Chuseok?
- How did your family celebrate Chuseok?
- How did you spend Chuseok?
- What did you do for/over Chuseok?

○ We visited our relatives.
○ We ate a lot of food.
○ I had a good time.

> **도움말**
>
> 대화 중 긍정문에서는 'much'보다는 'a lot'을 사용하는 것이 더 일반적입니다.

- What did you do last night?
- What did you do yesterday?
- Tell me what you did yesterday after school.
- Did you do anything special last night?

> **도움말**
>
> 다음 표현들을 활용하면 위의 문장을 좀 더 다양한 용도로 사용할 수 있습니다.
> on Saturday
> over the weekend
> on the weekend
> during the week
> the day before yesterday
> the day after tomorrow
> this morning

> **도움말**
>
> 'today morning'은 학생들이 간혹 사용할 수 있는 잘못된 표현입니다. 오늘 아침이라고 표현할 때는 'this morning'이라고 표현합니다.
>   incorrect: *today morning
>   correct: this morning

- I met Sun-mi yesterday.
- We had a baseball game.
- I went to a movie with some friends.

* What was it like?
* What happened?
* Did you have fun?
* Did you like/enjoy the show?
* Did you have a good time?

> **도움말**
>
> 'What was it like?'라는 표현으로 대화를 시작하지는 않습니다. 이 경우에는 'it'의 선행사가 필요합니다.

- I had a good time at the party.
- It was the best movie I've ever seen.

- Who won (the game)?
- Did you win?
- What was the score?
- How did your team do?

○ We won/lost.
○ The score was 3-0.

(사실이 아닌 것을 말한 후)
- That was a joke.
- Just kidding.
- I was just pulling your leg.

9 Responding
응답하기

> Student: Yesterday I went to the zoo.
> Teacher: Mm-hmm.
> Student: And one of the lions got out of the cage.
> Teacher: No way! Really?
> Student: It was this close to me.
> Teacher: Oh, my goodness!

- Mm-hmm.
- Oh, yeah?
- I see.
- That's interesting.

- I didn't know that.
- I never heard of that before.
- Well. That's different.

도움말

학생의 제반 학습 활동에 대한 교사의 반응은 학생의 학습을 강화하거나 약화시키는 데 큰 영향을 미칩니다. 그러므로 교사가 학생들에게 즉각적이고도 적절한 반응을 보여주는 것은 매우 중요합니다. 이 때 교사는 구두 언어(spoken language)와 몸짓 언어(body language)를 함께 사용할 수 있습니다. 위의 표현들은 상대방에게 반응을 보일 때 사용하는 구두 표현들입니다. 이러한 최소한의 반응은 교사가 학생의 이야기를 잘 듣고 있다는 표시가 되며, 이를 통하여 학생이 이

> 야기를 계속하도록 격려할 수 있습니다. 대화할 때에 이러한 최소한의 반응을 보여주는 것은 대화의 순조로운 진행에 많은 도움을 줍니다. TV 등의 대중 매체에서 'Oh, my God.'이라는 표현을 자주 사용하는데, 기독교인들은 그 표현을 거의 사용하지 않습니다.

- Are you sure?
- Really?
- Do you really think so?

○ I'm sure./No, not really.

- That's odd.
- That's surprising.
- I'm surprised you feel that way about it.

- Wow!
- That's great!
- That must have been exciting!
- You must be excited about it.

도움말

'exciting'은 사건을 묘사할 때 사용되고, 'excited'는 사람을 묘사할 때 사용합니다.

    incorrect: *You must have been exciting.
    correct: You must have been excited.

10 Date
날짜에 대하여 이야기하기

Teacher: What's the date today?
Student: It's March 29.
Teacher: And what day of the week is it?
Student: It's Monday.

- What's the date today?
- What's today's date?
- Is it the twenty-first or the twenty-second?

> **도움말**
>
> 관사와 소유대명사는 하나의 명사구에서 함께 사용될 수 없습니다.
> incorrect: *What's the today's date?
> correct: What's today's date?

- It's the twenty-first.
- It's September twenty-first.

> **도움말**
>
> 미국에서는 'September twenty-first, two thousand twelve(2012. 9.21.)'와 같이 날짜를 주로 달-일-년도의 순으로 표기합니다. 또는 'the twenty-first of September, two thousand twelve'라고 표현할 수도 있습니다.

I. The Beginning of the Lesson

- What day is it today?
- What day of the week is it?
- Is it Monday today?

○ It's Monday.

> **도움말**
>
> 다음은 학생들이 종종 틀리는 표현에 대한 예입니다.
> incorrect: *What day is today?
> correct: What day is it today?

11　Time
시간에 대하여 이야기하기

Teacher: What time is it?
Student: It's five o'clock.

- What time is it?
- Do you have the time?
- Do you have a watch?
- Got the time? (격식을 갖추지 않은 표현임)

◦ It's five o'clock.
◦ It's three twenty.
◦ It's twenty after three.
◦ It's twenty after.

12 Weather
날씨에 대하여 이야기하기

> Teacher: How's the weather today?
> Student: It's cold.
> Teacher: Is it still raining?
> Student: Yes, it is.

- How's the weather today?
- What's the weather like?
- What's it like outside?

  ○ It's raining/wet/snowing/freezing/sunny/hot/humid.
  ○ It's nice out.
  ○ It's a beautiful day.

- Is it raining outside?
- Is it still raining?
- Was it raining when you came in?

  ○ Yes./Yes, it is.
  ○ No, (it stopped.)

13 Compliments
칭찬하기

Teacher: Did you get your hair cut?
Student: Yes.
Teacher: That style looks nice on you.
Student: Thanks.

- Did you get a hair cut?
  ○ Yes, (I did.)/No, (I didn't.)
- Did you get your hair permed/straightened/dyed/styled?
  ○ Yes, (I did.)/No, (I didn't.)
- Your hair looks different today.
- You look like you have a new hair cut.

- Is that a new shirt?
  ○ Yes, (it is.)/No, (it isn't.)
- What a nice bag.
  ○ Thanks.
- Nice shirt. Is it new?
  ○ Yes, (it is.)/No, (it isn't.)
- Is that a new dress you have on?
  ○ Yes, (it is.)/No, (it isn't.)

- It looks nice on you.
- That style/color looks good on you.
- I like the color/style.
- It looks sharp.

  ◦ Thanks.
  ◦ Thanks a lot.
  ◦ Really? Thanks.
  ◦ I'm glad you like it.
  ◦ It's nice of you to say so.

14 Class Climate
교실 환경에 대하여 이야기하기

Teacher: I feel kind of cold. Are you cold?
Student: Yes, a little.
Teacher: Would you turn the heater up?
Student: Sure.

- It's hot/cold in here.
- Boy, it's hot.
- This room is kind of/a bit hot.
- Isn't it cold in here?
- I feel kind of cold. Are you cold?
- Don't you think it's too stuffy in here?
- It's too dark in here, isn't it?

> **도움말**
>
> 위의 표현들은 종종 완곡한 요청을 할 때 사용할 수 있습니다. 예를 들면 'Isn't it cold in here?'라고 말하여 누군가가 교실의 열린 창문을 닫도록 요청할 수 있습니다. 이러한 형태의 교실 영어 사용은 학생들이 영어 문장의 기능을 이해하는 데 도움을 줄 수 있습니다.

- Yes, it is.
- Yes, a little.
- No, it isn't.

I. The Beginning of the Lesson

- Would you mind if we had the door opened/closed?
- Is it okay if I open/close the window?
- Would it be all right if I put my coat on/took my jacket off?
- Would it bother you if we had the heater on/off/up/down?

> **도움말**
>
> 교사가 학생에게 영어로 불을 켜 달라고 하거나 창문을 열어 달라고 하는 등의 도움을 요청하는 것은, 학생에게 부탁을 하는 동시에 학생이 실제 상황에서 영어를 사용할 수 있는 기회를 제공하는 것이 됩니다.

- Sure.
- Go ahead.
- Fine with me.

> **도움말**
>
> 다음을 활용하면 위의 표현들을 다양한 용도로 사용할 수 있습니다.
> draw the curtains
> let the blinds down
> open/close/shut the window
> open/close/shut the door
> pull the shade/blinds
> put on/take off a jacket

> **도움말**
>
> vertical blinds와 curtains의 경우 drawn, opened, closed와 같은 동사들과 같이 사용되며, horizontal blinds은 pulled라는 표현과 함께 사용됩니다. 'close the blinds', 'let the (horizontal) blinds down', 'close the (vertical) blinds (by drawing them across the window)', 'turn the angle of the blinds to block out more light' 등의 표현을 함께 알아두면 좋습니다.

- The fan would help.
- It would be nice to have the fan on.
- We could use some circulation in here.

- We don't need the air-conditioner.
- I think we'll feel better without the air-conditioner.
- It's too cold in here with the air-conditioner on.

- Can you see all right?
  ◦ Yes, I can./No, I can't.
- Do you need more light to work?
  ◦ Yes, (I do.)/No, that's all right.
- Can you work without the light?
  ◦ Yes, I'm okay./No, not really.
- Is the sun getting in your eyes?
  ◦ Yes, kind of./No, it's okay.

- Would you do me a favor?
- Help me, please.
- Could you give me a hand?
- Would you mind helping us out?
- Chan-hee, I have a job for you.

○ Sure.
○ No problem.
○ What do you need?
○ Just a minute.

- Could you turn on the lights?
- Can someone open the door?
- Mail this letter for me, will you?
- Would you please help me move this desk?
- Can you open the window please?

> **도움말**
>
> 교실에서 종종 사용되는 틀린 표현의 예입니다.
> awkward: *Can anyone open the door?
> correct: Can someone open the door?

○ Okay. I'll do it.
○ (I've) got it.
○ Sorry. I can't.
○ I'm afraid I can't.

- Please, turn your cellphones off during class.
- Don't let your phone go off during class.
- Cellphones should be turned off before you come to class. If your phone rings, I'll mark you absent.

> **도움말**
>
> 핸드폰에 대한 미국영어와 영국영어의 차이, 그리고 틀린 표현의 예입니다.
>
> American English: cellphone, smartphone
> British English: mobile phone
> incorrect: *hand phone

15 Checking Homework
숙제 점검하기

Teacher: Take out your homework.
Student: What was the assignment?
Teacher: The worksheet I gave you yesterday. Remember? I'd like to collect the homework now. Could you pass your papers to the front?

- What was your homework from last time?
- What did I ask you to do for today?
- What were you supposed to bring today?

○ What was the assignment?

- Did everyone bring a family picture?
- Do you all have a family picture with you?
- Did you all remember to bring a family picture today?

- Take out your homework.
- Could you find your homework?
- Please get your homework out.

- Let me check your homework.
- I'll come around the room and check your homework.
- Put your assignment on your desk and I'll look at it.
- Get your homework out so I can come around and check it.

- Write your name at the top.
- Don't forget to put your name at the top.
- Make sure your name is on your paper.

- Give me your homework, please.
- I'd like to collect the homework now.
- Could you hand in your assignment?
- It's time to turn in the homework.

> **도움말**
>
> 교사가 한 학생에게 숙제 걷는 것을 부탁하는 경우에 'Everyone, collect your assignments.'라고 하는 것은 틀린 표현입니다. 이러한 경우에는 'Give your assignments to me.' 혹은 'Give your assignments to Yoon-ju.'라고 말하는 것이 적절합니다.

- Pass your homework forward.
- Could you hand your papers to the front (of the room)?
- Please, send your assignments to your right.

> **도움말**
>
> 교사가 숙제를 걷을 때 'Pass your papers forward.', 혹은 'Hand your papers to the front.' 와 같은 표현을 사용 할 수 있습니다. 만약 학생을 통하여 걷을 경우는 'Hand the papers to (student's name).' 라고 말할 수 있습니다.
>
> | Pass | your homework | in. |
> | Hand | your papers | to the front. |
> | | your assignments | forward. |
> | | | to your right/left. |
> | | | to me. |
> | | | to Jeong-min. |

- Do you want our assignments now?
- Should I give this to you now?

* Don't turn it in now. I'll take it later.
* Wait until the end of class, and then turn in your assignment.
* I don't need it just yet. Why don't you give it to me at the end of class.

* Please hand in your homework before you leave.
* Please give your homework to me on your way out.
* Don't forget to give me your homework before you go.

- Here.
- Here it is.

16 Review of the Previous Lesson
이전 수업 내용 복습하기

Teacher:	Let's review. Do you remember what we talked about last time? We talked about ...
Student 1:	Jobs?
Teacher:	Yes, we talked about jobs.
Student 2:	Oh, yeah.
Teacher:	What do you say when you want to find out someone's job?

- Shall we start off with a song?
- Let's warm up with the song we learned yesterday.
- Let's start with a little review.
- Let's begin by going over the expressions we practiced yesterday.
- To start off, let's review yesterday's lesson.

- Let's review.
- Let's review what we did yesterday.
- Shall we go over it again?
- Why don't we do this one more time?
- Let's do it again, all right?
- Maybe we can do a little review.

I. The Beginning of the Lesson

- What did we do last time?
- What do you remember about ... ?
- Do you remember what we talked about last time?
- What words did we learn last time?

- We talked about jobs.
- We practiced asking people about their jobs.
- We learned how to ask people about their jobs.

> **도움말**
>
> 교사들은 종종 문장의 끝을 비워둠으로써 학생이 빈칸을 채울 수 있는 기회를 줄 수 있습니다. 'We talked about ...' 혹은 'We learned how to ask people about ... what?'등이 그 예입니다.

- Last time we were practicing giving directions.
- We have been studying giving directions, right? Right.
- Let's see how much you can remember about giving directions.

- Let's practice giving directions again.
- Today we'll do a little more with directions.
- We are going to continue working on directions, like we did last time.
- We did this last time.
- I think we went over this last week.
- You had this in your last class.

- Remember this?
- We did this last time. Right? Right.
- Remember this expression?
- We practiced this expression last week, didn't we?

> **도움말**
>
> 'right?' 혹은 'didn't we?'와 같은 부가의문문은 교사가 동의를 구할 때 사용되는 것으로 학생이 대답할 수 있고 확인할 수 있는 기회를 제공합니다. 학생이 단지 웃거나 고개를 끄덕이는 행동을 보인다면 교사가 아래와 같은 반응으로 확인해 줄 수 있습니다.
>
> For example:
>   Teacher: Remember this?
>   Students: (nodding) Ahh.
>   Teacher: (nodding) Oh, yeah.

(기억이 되살아남을 알릴 때)
- Oh, yeah. (I remember.)
- That's right. I remember now.

I. The Beginning of the Lesson

17. Transition to New Work
새로운 수업 내용으로 이동하기

> Teacher: It looks like we're ready to begin. Let's start where we left off last time. What page were we on? Did we finish page 20 on Monday?
> Student: Yes, I think so.
> Teacher: Good.

- Shall we get started?
- Shall we begin?
- Are you ready?
- Let's get started.
- I think we can get started.
- It looks like we're ready to begin.
- Let's get down to work.

도움말

'Let's start.'라는 표현보다는 'Shall we get started?' 나 'Let's get started.' 라는 표현이 더 자연스럽습니다.

- Let's continue with what we were doing last time.
- First we'll finish up what we began last class.
- We'll start where we left off last time.

- Where were we last time? Page 20./I don't remember.
- Where did we stop? Page 20./I don't remember.
- What page were we on? Page 20./I don't remember.
- How far did we get last time? Page 20./I don't remember.
- What was the last thing we did. Do you remember? Yes./No, I don't know.
- Do you remember where we finished on Monday? Page 20. /I don't remember.

- Last time we got to page 20.
- We were on page 20 before, weren't we? Yes. I think so./ No, we were on page 19.
- We we're working on page 20 when we stopped last time. Yes. I think so./No, we were on page 19.
- Did we make it up to page 20 on Monday? Yes. I think so./ No, we were on page 19.

도움말

교사가 무엇에 관하여 물어보는 것은 학생들에게 답을 할 수 있는 기회를 제공하는 것입니다. 교사가 'Last time we got to page twenty.'라고 말하면 학생들에게 아무런 대화가 일어나지 않을 수 있지만, 지난 수업에서 어디까지 배웠는지를 물어본다면 학생들은 교사의 기억을 돕고자 응답에 적극적으로 참여할 것입니다.

18 Seating Arrangements
자리 정리하기

Teacher: Could you straighten up the desks?
Student: Is this good?
Teacher: Okay, but let's make an aisle here. We need enough room for someone to walk through here.

- Straighten your desks, please.
- Make sure your desks are straight.
- Let's put the chairs in nice, straight rows.

- Let's make an aisle here.
- Leave a space between these two rows.
- We need enough room for someone to walk through here.

- Let's put 4 chairs together in each group.
- Could you push the desks into groups of 4?
- We need to move the desks. 4 chairs in a group.

- Let's make a big circle.
- Put all of the chairs in a circle.
- I would like you to put all of your chairs in a big circle.
- Make a round circle.
- Well, this is really more of an oval.
- Could you bring those chairs into the circle too?

> **도움말**
> 교사가 자리 배치(seating arrangements)를 지시할 때 제스처를 사용하는 것이 좋습니다. 학생들이 교사의 지시를 친숙하게 이해할 수 있는 방법은 제스처를 사용하는 것입니다.

- Like this?
- Is this good?

19 Getting Out School Supplies
수업 자료 꺼내기

> Teacher: Please, get out your books. Where's your book? Did you forget it?
> Student: It's at home.
> Teacher: Well, don't forget again, okay?
> Student: Yes.
> Teacher: You better share with Min-ho.

- Get your books.
- Find your English books.
- Please, get out your English books.
- Could you take your English books out?

◦ Which book?
◦ This book?

- You only need your English book.
- Put all your other books and papers away.
- We're not working with that book right now.
- You don't need that book. Just your English book.

- Where's your book?
- Don't you have one?
- Didn't you bring yours?
- Did you forget yours?

- Did you leave it at home?

◦ I lost it.
◦ I can't find it.
◦ It's at home.

> **도움말**
>
> 교사는 좀 더 수준 높은 언어의 모범을 보이기 위하여 학생들의 영어를 종종 좀 더 길게 부연하여 말해주기도 합니다.
> For example:
>   Teacher: Where's your book?
>   Student: Home.
>   Teacher: Oh, it's at home.

- Don't forget again. Okay?
- Try to remember it next time.
- Make sure you have it on Friday.
- Be sure to bring it next time.

- You better share with Min-ho.
- You'll have to share with your neighbor, won't you?
- I guess you'll have to look on with Jang-san.
- Son-ha, can she look on with you?

- Who can share a pencil with Chong-beom? I can.
- Is there anyone who has an extra pencil? I do.
- Do you have a pen? Yes./No.
- Is there anyone who can lend Joon-gyu a pencil just for today?

> **도움말**
>
> 'lend'와 'borrow'라는 단어의 사용에 유의할 필요가 있습니다. 'lend'는 당분간 빌려 주는 것이고, 'borrow'는 당분간 빌려오는 것입니다.
>
> incorrect: *Is there anyone who can borrow Joon-gyu a pencil?
> correct: Is there anyone who can lend Joon-gyu a pencil?

- I lost my book.
- I think I left my book here last time.
- I forgot where I put my book.

> **도움말**
>
> 관사와 소유격은 함께 사용하지 않음을 학생들에게 알려줄 필요가 있습니다.
>
> incorrect: *I lost the my book.
> correct: I lost my book.

- Where did you put it? Over there./In my backpack./On the table.
- Where did you last have it? At home.
- When did you see it last? Yesterday./Last night.
- Do you remember where you left it? Over there./In my back pack./On the table.

- I'll tell you if I see it.
- I'll keep an eye out for it.
- I'll let you know if it shows up.

- Thanks.

- Has anyone found a book?
- Did anyone see a book?
- Has anyone seen Il-hyun's book?

◦ It's over there.
◦ I saw it in the hallway.
◦ Here it is.

- Who lost a pencil? I did./Maybe Yong-eun did.
- Did anyone lose a pencil? I did./He did.
- Is anyone missing a pencil? I am./She is.

- Whose pencil?
- Whose pencil is this?
- Does this pencil belong to anyone?
- Is this your book?

◦ Yeah, that's mine.
◦ That's Dae-won's.

20 Distribution of New Materials
새로운 수업 자료 배부하기

I have some pictures today.
I've brought some magazines for you.
We'll be working with these things today.

도움말

'prepare'의 오용 사례입니다.
　　awkward: *I prepared some magazines for you.
　　correct:　 I brought some magazines for you.

- These handouts are about...
- These are pictures of...
- These things have to do with...
- This article shows/tells you something about...

- I put the cards over there.
- You can pick up the worksheets here.
- The handouts are over there.

- What do we do with these?
- How do we use the cards?

- You can put the card up here.
- Stick the card on the wall.
- Put the poster up here.

- Can you see the picture?
- Can you all see it now?
- Is that good?

> **도움말**
>
> 'see'와 'look at'은 그 의미에 있어서 차이가 있습니다. 'see'라는 동사는 볼 수 있는 능력을 나타내며(Can you see the picture?), look at은 집중해서 봐달라는 요청의 의미를 가집니다(Can you 'look at' the picture?). 그러므로 첫 번째 질문의 답으로는 'Yes./No.'가 가능 지만, 두 번째 질문에 대해서는 동의(agree)와 부동의(disagree)로 답해야 합니다.

○ Yes. That's okay.
○ I can't really see it.

- Here are some new worksheets.
- I have some new worksheets for you.
- I have some worksheets to hand out today.

- Pass these around.
- Take one and pass them on.
- Please take a copy and hand the rest back.

> **도움말**
>
> 'Please take a copy and hand the rest back.'이라는 문장은 worksheet를 나눠줄 때 첫 번째 줄에 앉은 학생들이 뒤에 앉은 학생들에게 전달하라는 의미입니다. 'Pass these around.'는 paper를 어떠한 지시가 없이 자유롭게 나눠줄 때 사용할 수 있는 표현입니다.

I. The Beginning of the Lesson | 65

- Jeong-mi, would you hand these out?
- Seon-yeong, would you pass these around?
- Could you give a copy to everyone?

○ Okay.
○ Sure.

- One each.
- Give one to each person.
- Each person gets one.

- There are 2 different sheets.
- You need to have 2 different papers.
- Make sure you have both papers. One looks like this, and one looks like this.

○ I need the other sheet.
○ I only got one paper.

- Does everyone have a copy?
- Does anyone need a copy?
- Can everyone see a copy?
- Is there anyone who doesn't have a copy?

> **도움말**
>
> 'everyone', 'anyone' 과 'a copy'는 모두 단수입니다. 그러므로 동사도 역시 단수 주어와 일치시켜 주어야 합니다. 따라서 'Do everyone have a copy?' 는 틀린 표현이 됩니다.

- I need one.
- I didn't get one.
- Min-jun needs a copy yet.

* There aren't enough copies for the whole class.
* Oh dear. We're a few copies short.
* I'm afraid there aren't enough to go around.

* We'll have to share. 2 to a copy.
* 1 copy for every 2 people.
* You'll have to share with the person sitting next to you.

> **도움말**
>
> 교실은 한 장소를 의미하므로 'whole'과 'class'가 함께(the whole class) 쓰입니다. 하지만 학생들의 경우는 한 명이 아니고 많은 학생들이므로 'whole students'는 올바른 표현이 아닙니다. 올바른 표현은 'all of the students'입니다.

* Are there any extras?
* Could I have the extra papers?
* Would you hand the extra papers over here?

- Here.
- I have some.
- What do I do with these/the extras?

* Please don't write on these. I need them back.
* Be careful with these. I want them back at the end of class.
* You'll have to give them back at the end of the lesson.
* I need to use these again, so please don't fold them.

- ◦ Can we keep these?
- ◦ Can I take it home?

- I'd like you to take these to class again next time.
- You may keep these, but please bring them back next time.
- Hang onto these. Don't lose them.

PART II

The Development of the Lesson
수업 전개

PART II
The Development of the Lesson
수업 전개

1. Introducing the Subject/Course 과목/강의 소개하기
2. Introducing Today's Lesson 오늘의 수업 소개하기
3. Sequencing 수업 내용의 순서 정하기
4. Moving On 수업 진도 나가기
5. Taking a Break 휴식 시간 갖기
6. Starting Again/Back to Work 수업 다시 시작하기
7. Using Korean/English 한국어/영어 사용하기
8. Student Presentation 학생 발표하기
9. Repetition and Responses 반복 및 응답하기
10. Choral Response 전체 반복 및 응답하기
11. Individual Response 개인 응답하기
12. Taking Turns 순서 교체하기
13. Class in Halves 분반하기
14. Individual Work 개인 활동하기
15. Pairwork 짝 활동하기
16. Group Work 그룹 활동하기
17. Dividing into Teams 팀 나누기
18. Asking for Volunteers 자원자 요청하기
19. Movement, General Activity 동작, 일반 활동하기
20. Leaving the Classroom 교실 나가기
21. Checking Comprehension 이해력 점검하기

22. Asking for Clarification 설명 요청하기
23. Giving Feedback 피드백 제공하기
24. Confirmation 확인하기
25. Leading to the Answer 정답 유도하기
26. Encouragement 격려하기
27. Evaluation 평가하기
28. Giving Opinions 의견 제시하기
29. Showing Preference 선호하는 것 제시하기
30. Explaining and Giving Examples 설명 및 예시하기
31. Class Control and Discipline 수업 통제하기 및 훈육하기
32. Establishing Rules 규칙 설정하기
33. Getting Attention 주의 집중시키기
34. Warning 경고하기
35. Giving Permission 허락하기
36. Apologizing 사과하기
37. Offering Help 도움주기
38. Thanking 감사하기
39. Giving 나누기
40. Congratulating/Well Wishing 축하/축복하기

1 Introducing the Subject/Course
과목/강의 소개하기

> Teacher: Welcome to English I. This is a required course, but General English is a prerequisite for this class. So if you're here and you haven't taken General English yet, you are in the wrong place. I brought the syllabus for you. Would you each take a copy of the syllabus? Let me show you the textbook. We'll be using *Behavior in Organizations* by Kim, Seong Kuk. The publisher is Sunhak-sa. Please get a copy this week and bring it with you the next time we meet. It should be available in the bookstore.

- This is a required/elective course.
- Everyone/not everyone has to take this class.
- This class is mandatory/optional.

- You need to take General English before you take English I.
- Normally students need to take General English before enrolling in this class.
- General English is a prerequisite for this class.

- I brought the syllabus for you. Take one and pass them on.
- Would you each take a copy of the syllabus?
- Here are the syllabuses. You may each take one.

- Let me show you the textbook.

II. The Development of the Lesson

- This is the book we will be using for the course.
- We'll be referring to this book through out the course.

- Don't share books. You need to buy your own book.
- You'll need to get your own copy of this book.
- You should pick up a copy at the bookstore.
- Please get a copy this week and bring it with you next time.

- The title of the book is *Behavior in Organizations*.
- We'll be using *Behavior in Organizations* by Kim Seong Kuk.
- The textbook for the course is *Behavior in Organizations* by Kim Seong Kuk.
- It was written by Kim Seong-kook and published by Sunhak-Sa.
- The publisher is Sunhak-Sa.

> **도움말**
>
> 글을 통하여 영어책의 제목을 소개할 때에는 일반적으로 밑줄을 긋거나 이탤릭체로 표시해줍니다. 단원(chapter)이나 글의 제목은 따옴표(' ') 표시를 해줍니다.

- It's a very recent book— it was just published last year.
- It came out last year/in 2011.
- The publication date is 2011.

- Make sure you get the third edition.
- You need to have the most recent edition.
- If you have a different edition, your page numbers will be different from the rest of ours.

- I'd like to recommend some supplementary reading for this course.
- I encourage you to take a look at this website when you have time.
- Here are several books, economic newspapers, journals, and websites that you should be familiar with.

> **도움말**
>
> 'recommend' 와 'encourage' 라는 단어의 쓰임에 대하여 주의를 기울일 필요가 있습니다. 제안을 할 때 아래와 같은 형식으로 사용 할 수 있습니다.
> I recommend (noun): I recommend these books.
> I recommend (gerund): I recommend reading these books.
> I recommend that you (infinitive): I recommend that you read these books.
> I encourage you to (infinitive): I encourage you to read these books.
> I encourage (gerund): I encourage reading.
> 마지막 문장인 'I encourage (gerund).'은 특정한 요청을 할 때 보다는 일반적인 제안을 할 때 사용하는 것입니다.

- I've written them down on the syllabus.
- You can find them listed on the syllabus.
- I won't read all of the titles now, but you'll see them on the second page of your syllabus.

- I have put these books on reserve in the library.
- This book should be available in the bookstore.
- You can pick up a copy in the bookstore.

- Each member of the group should participate.
- The work should be divided among all the members of your group.
- Make sure each person in your group carries his or her own weight.

- Participation is a very important part of your grade.
- Participation will count as 30% of your total score.
- Participation is weighted heavily in your total score.

- Degree of preparation and of completeness will be 40%.

- I will also consider how well you use multimedia equipment — such as PPT and video — in your presentation.
- Part of your grade is based on how well you use multi-media equipment.

- Presentation technique will count 30%.
- I will be looking very closely at your presentation technique.
- Your presentation technique is also a significant part of your grade.

- The final examination is worth 30% of your grade.
- The midterm and the final are each worth 30% of your grade.
- The midterm and the final exams together make up 60% of your grade.

- The group presentation will count as 20% of your grade.
- Homework makes up 10%.
- Attendance is 20% of your grade.

도움말

일반적으로 첫 강의를 할 때 교사가 학생들의 결석이나 지각과 관련한 규칙을 소개합니다. 다음은 대학 강의의 한 예입니다.

For example:

Attendance counts as 20% of your grade. ANY STUDENT MISSING 4 OR MORE CLASSES WILL RECEIVE AN F in the course. Missing a 50 minute class counts as one day's absence. Missing a 100 minute class counts as two days' absence. This is the lateness policy. Students who arrive within the first 10 minutes after the class starts will be marked LATE. Three LATE marks count as an absence. Students arriving more than 10 minutes late will be marked absent for the class.

2 Introducing Today's Lesson
오늘의 수업 소개하기

> Today we're going to practice ...
> Today we're going to learn about ...
> This is what we're going to talk about today.
> Our goal today is to learn how to ...
> By the end of class today, I want you to be able to ...

도움말

아래의 표현들이 어떻게 사용되는지 알아봅시다.

practice (thing): We're going to practice a song.
practice (gerund/activity): We're going to practice giving directions.
learn about (topic): We're going to learn about global warming.
learn how to (infinitive/activity): We're going to learn how to write business letters.
be able to (infinitive/activity): I want you to be able to say this from memory.

- I'm going to talk about ...
- I'll tell you about ...
- I'm going to go over some information about ...

3 Sequencing
수업 내용의 순서 정하기

> Teacher: To start off, I'd like you to read the passage on page 80. Then fill in the blanks at the bottom of the page. In a few minutes, we'll go over the answers as a class.

- First let's ...
- First of all, we'll ...
- To start off, I'd like you to ...
- The first time you may ...
- Let's start off with some ... ing.

도움말

'from now on' 이라는 표현을 사용할 때는 주의가 필요합니다. 이 표현은 미래에 어떤 일이 지속적으로 일어날 것임을 나타낼 때 사용됩니다. 그러므로 'I want you to hand in your homework on time from now on.'이라고 말하는 것은 괜찮으나, 'We are going to practice a conversation from now on.' 이라고 말하는 것은 적절하지 않습니다. 왜냐하면 이 말은 당신이 회화 연습을 전혀 중단하지 않고 계속할 것이라는 의미를 담고 있기 때문입니다.

◦ I'm finished. What do I do now?

- Next, I'd like you to ...
- Then ...
- And then ...

II. The Development of the Lesson

- After that, we'll ...
- After you're done, ...
- When we've finished this, we'll ...
- Later on, we're going to ...

- Finally, we'll ...
- At the end of class, we'll ...
- Just before we go, we're going to...
- When are we going to play the game?

(시간을 나타낼 때)
- in a few minutes
- in a half hour
- after the break
- when class ends
- at the end of class

> **도움말**
>
> 'a few minutes after'는 잘못된 표현입니다. 'in a few minutes' 가 맞는 표현입니다.
>
> incorrect: *a few minutes after
> correct: in a few minutes

- How much time do we have?

- I'll give you 10 minutes.
- You should finish this in 10 minutes.
- After 10 minutes, we're going to move on to something else.

- You have to finish by 10:30.
- We're going to stop at 10:30.
- I'll give you until 10:30 to finish this up.

- 5 seconds.
- I'll give you 5 seconds to finish up.
- You have 5 seconds left.

> **도움말**
>
> 5부터 1까지 거꾸로 숫자를 세는 것은 어린 학습자에게 효과적인 학습 방법입니다. 교사는 다음과 같이 말할 수 있습니다.
>
> 'Five! Four! Three! Two! One! One half! One quarter! Hurry up, last chance! And stop!'

4 Moving On
수업 진도 나가기

> Teacher: Okay. That's enough. Stop what you're working on.
> Student: Just a minute.
> Teacher: Time to wrap it up.
> Student: Okay.
> Teacher: Let's move on to the next thing.

- Okay!
- All right!
- That's good!
- That's enough!

- Stop what you're doing.
- Time to wrap it up.
- Finish up what you're working on.

◦ Wait.
◦ Just a minute.
◦ I'm not done yet.
◦ Okay.

- We need some practice with that.
- Let's practice what we just learned.
- Why don't we practice for a few minutes?

> **도움말**
> 'practice'는 불가산 명사입니다.
>   incorrect: *We need some practices.
>   correct: We need some practice.

- We've had enough practice with that.
- I think we're ready to move on.
- I think you've gotten the hang of that.
- Let's move on to the next thing.
- Let's do something else.
- It's time to move on to something new.
- We should go on to something else now.

- OK, it's time to go over the answers together.
- Let's move on to some reading.
- Now I think we're ready to practice the conversation.
- Now, let's look at the dialogue on page 12.

- I hate to stop you, but we have to go on.
- I know you don't want to stop, but we have to move on.
- I know you're having fun, but we have other exciting things to do.

- Don't stop.
- Please, keep going.
- Keep working until I stop you.
- When you're finished, do another one.

5 Taking a Break
휴식 시간 갖기

Teacher: Okay. Break time. We'll start again in 5 minutes.

- Break time.
- Let's take a break.
- I'll give you a 5 minute break.
- Okay, you can relax for a few minutes.

- We'll start again in 5 minutes.
- Come back in 5 minutes.
- Be back here in 5 minutes.
- You should be ready to start working again at 10:15.

- I'd like to talk to you during the break.
- Could you talk to me during the break?
- I'd like to see you for a minute.

6 Starting Again/Back to Work
수업 다시 시작하기

> Students: (chanting) Whether the weather be fine or whether the weather be not, we'll weather the weather, whatever the weather whether we like it or not.
> Teacher: Let's do it again but this time, I want to hear a clear 'w' on 'we'll weather.' Let's take it from the top.
> Students: Whether the weather ...

- Let's do it again, but this time...
- Would you mind starting over?
- I think we better start over.
- I want you to go back to the beginning.
- Let's take it from the top.

- Where were we?
- I lost my train of thought. What were we doing just now?
- What was I saying before we were interrupted?

- Back to work.
- Now we'll go back to what we were doing before.
- All right. Let's go on with what we were doing.

7 Using Korean/English
한국어/영어 사용하기

> Teacher: What's this?
> Student: 나비.
> Teacher: Right. Now how do you say that in English?

- What's ... in Korean/in English?
- How do you say... in Korean/in English?
- What's the Korean/English word for ... ?
- How would you say ... in Korean/in English?
- I'll say the word in English and you say it in Korean.
- When I say a word in English, you respond with the Korean word.
- When you hear the English word, say the Korean word.

- Translate this sentence into English.
- Translate from Korean to English.
- Could you put this in English?
- Right. Now how do you say that in English?
- Exactly. Say the same thing, this time in English.
- Good. What do you call that in English?

> **도움말**
>
> 학생이 영어를 사용하지 않을 때에도 교사가 영어로 정답을 확인시켜 주는 것이 좋습니다. 이것은 학생들이 영어로 대답하는 방법을 알아내는 데 도움을 줄 수 있습니다. 학생들이 영어로 대답하기 어려워하는 경우에는 교사가 번역하여 주거나 적절한 영어 표현을 알려 줄 수 있습니다.

- Use English.
- Use English only.
- Try it in English, please.
- Say it in English, please.

- Please don't translate.
- Don't explain in Korean.
- Try to do the whole thing in English.
- You can do this in English.
- You don't need to translate.
- I know you can understand this in English.

- I want you to listen to the English.
- I want you to understand it in English.
- Listen carefully. You can understand it.

> **도움말**
>
> 위 문장들은 학생들이 들리는 영어를 이해하려 하기보다 우선 번역을 하고자 할 때 사용할 수 있는 표현입니다. 이와 같은 표현을 자주 사용하면서 직청직해를 강조하면 효과적인 듣기 학습을 유도할 수 있습니다.

8. Student Presentation
학생 발표하기

> Teacher: Min-ho and Sunju, can you demonstrate for us?
> Students: Okay.
> Teacher: Thanks. Come up to the front please.

- Can you demonstrate for us?
- I'd like you to demonstrate what we've been working on.
- Would you be willing to show us what you've done?

- That's all. Thanks.
- That's good. Thank you.
- You're done. Good job.

- You may sit down.
- You can sit down again.
- You may go back to your seat.

- Come here, please.
- Come up to the front, please.
- Would you come up to the front?

9 Repetition and Responses
반복 및 응답하기

> Teacher: Repeat after me: 'Peter Piper picked a peck of pickled peppers.'
> Students: Peter... Piper.
> Teacher: All of you. Listen and then say it how I say it. 'Pickled peppers.'
> Students: 'Pickled peppers.'
> Teacher: 'A peck of pickled peppers.'
> Students: 'A peck of pickled peppers.'

- Repeat after me.
- Listen and repeat.
- I'll say it and then you say it.

10 Choral Response
전체 반복 및 응답하기

Teacher: pickled peppers
Students: pickled peppers
Teacher: a peck of pickled peppers
Students: a peck of pickled peppers
Teacher: picked a peck of pickled peppers...

- All of you.
- The whole class, together.
- All together now...
- Everyone say, 'She went to ...'
- Say it all together.

> **도움말**
>
> 학급 전체가 한 목소리로 말하도록 유도할 때는 명령어 'tell'이 아니라 'say'를 사용합니다. 'say'는 학생들이 똑같은 말을 하도록 요구하지만 'tell'은 그렇지 않습니다.
>
> 'say'는 직접 목적어를 취합니다. 종종 'say'의 직접 목적어는 quotation인 경우가 많습니다. 'Say it all together.'라는 문장에서 'it'는 quotation을 가리킵니다. 'Say all together.'는 직접 목적어가 없으므로 틀린 표현입니다.

- I'd like you all to answer the question.
- I want the whole class to answer the question.
- Could all of you answer the question?

> **도움말**
>
> 제안할 때는 'I'd like + 사람 + to + 부정사' 와 'I want + 사람 + to + 부정사' 와 같이 전치사 'to'를 반드시 포함시켜야 합니다. 제안하는 표현으로 'I'd like (person) to (infinitive)' 와 'I want (person) to (infinitive)'를 사용할 수 있습니다.

- You too, Su-pil.
- You join in this time, Chong-won.
- Let's do it again with Sun-yeong.

11 Individual Response
개인 응답하기

Teacher: Jin-hee, could you do it by yourself?
Students: She wanted to ...
Teacher: Just Jin-hee. Don't give her the answer.
Jin-hee: She wanted to study hard.

- Just Min-jung.
- Okay. Kyung-hee, your turn.
- Let's hear Sung-jin alone.
- Jin-hee, could you do it by yourself?

- Don't help him.
- It's Sung-min's turn.
- Don't give him the answer.
- Let him figure it on his own.
- I'm sure he can do it by himself.

12 Taking Turns
순서 교체하기

Teacher:	Let's take turns. We'll go around the room and give everyone a chance. Bo-ra, would you start?
Bo-ra:	I'm going on a picnic and I'm taking an apple.
Teacher:	Good. Next?
Chang-won:	I'm going on a picnic and I'm taking an apple and some cookies.
Teacher:	Who's next.
Bo-ra:	It's Jong-heop's turn.

- 1 at a time.
- Not altogether.
- Let's take turns.
- Do this 1 at a time.
- We'll go around the room and give everyone a chance.

> **도움말**
>
> 학생들이 연속 활동에 익숙하지 않을 때는 몸동작을 사용하여 시각적인 방법으로 설명해 주는 것이 도움이 될 수 있습니다.
> Teacher: (첫 학생을 가리키며) It's your turn first. (두번째 학생을 바라보며) You're second. (세번째 학생을 바라보며) And then it's your turn and so on around the room.

- You go first.
- It's your turn first.
- Why don't you start?

- Whose turn is it?
- Is it your turn?
- Who's next?
- Who's up?
- Where are we?

◦ It's my turn.
◦ It's Jeong-hyop's turn.
◦ It's her turn.

- Min-uk first.
- Bo-ra, would you start?
- We'll start with Jae-won.
- Woo-hye, could you go first?
- Dae-hyun, why don't you start us off?

- Good. Next?
- Who's next?
- Fine. Now it's your turn.
- All right. Kil-jin just went. Now it's Sun-ju's turn.
- Good work, Kil-jin. Now, Sun-ju?

- You've already had a turn.
- You've done this already.
- You've tried it once already.
- You already went.

- Wait your turn.
- Let someone else have a turn.
- Don't answer everything yourself.
- Give someone else a chance.

- Have you all had a turn?
- Has everyone answered at least once?
- Is there anyone who hasn't had a chance yet?

- Who's left?
- Who else is there?
- Who hasn't had a turn yet?

○ I haven't gone yet.
○ Myung-ju hasn't had a turn.

○ How do I do it?
○ What am I supposed to do?

- Do it the same way.
- Now you do the same thing.
- Do it just like he did.

> **도움말**
>
> 'same' 앞에는 정관사 'the'를 반드시 사용해야 합니다.
>   incorrect: *Do it same way.
>   correct: Do it the same way.

- Don't let Hyun-jin answer all the questions.
- Someone else should give it a try.
- Let's hear from someone else.

13 Class in Halves
분반하기

> Teacher: Let's split right down the middle. You on this side read part A. You on this side read part B. Part A, ready? Go.

- Now, I'll divide you in half.
- First, I'm going to divide you down the middle.
- Let's split right down the middle, between Su-min and Yong-tae.
- You on this side read part A. You on this side read part B.
- Everyone on this side, up to Yong-ah, read part A. And starting with Jin-ah, you read part B.
- If you're on the window side of the room, read part A. If you sit by the door, read part B.

- I want this half to read the next sentence.
- I'd like that half to continue reading.
- Could this half of the room read the next part?

- Women/Men only.
- We'll have all the women/men do it this time.
- Let's hear the women/men only this time.
- Just the women/men, please.

도움말

초등학교의 경우 교사는 학생들을 'boys and girls'라고 부르며, 고등학교와 대학교에서는 'men and women'이라고 부르는 것이 일반적입니다.

14 Individual Work
개인 활동하기

Teacher: Please work by yourselves now.
After a minute you can talk about it with a partner.

- Work on your own.
- Work by yourselves.
- Everybody work individually.
- Try to work independently.
- I want you to work on your own.

15 Pairwork
짝 활동하기

Teacher: I'd like you to do this in pairs, so find a partner.
Student: I don't have a partner.
Teacher: So-ra doesn't have a partner either. Could you ask her to work with you?
Student: So-ra, do you want to work with me?
So-ra: Okay.

- We'll do some pairwork now.
- Let's do some pairwork.
- I have a pair activity for you to do today.

도움말

'group work'와 같이 pairwork은 불가산 명사지만 'pair activity'는 가산 명사입니다.
　　incorrect: *Let's do a pairwork.
　　correct:　 Let's do a pair activity.

- In pairs.
- Work in pairs.
- In groups of 2.
- Get into pairs.
- I'd like you to do this in pairs.
- Work in groups of 2.

- Find a partner.
- Work together with a friend.
- Why don't you work with the person sitting next to you?

- Do you have a partner?
- Do you need a partner?
- Do you want to work with me (us)?
- Does everyone have a partner?

○ I don't have a partner.
○ I don't have anyone to work with.

> **도움말**
>
> 짝 활동을 위하여 파트너를 찾게 하는 것은 학생들에게 교실영어 연습을 할 수 있는 좋은 기회를 제공합니다. 학생들이 짝 활동을 위해 파트너를 편안하게 선택할 수 있도록 'Do you have a partner?' 같은 표현을 학생들에게 미리 가르쳐 주면 도움이 될 것입니다.

- Why don't you two work together?
- Could you be partners?
- So-ra doesn't have a partner either. Could you ask her to work with you?

- Work with the person behind/in front of/next to you.
- Turn around and face the person behind you.

- Person A starts.
- Person A goes first.
- Person A starts off with the first question and person B answers.

- This time work with someone new.
- Stand up and find a new partner.
- Find someone you haven't worked with before today.
- You've already worked with Sin-ah. You need a new partner.

- Each pair should join another pair to make a group of 4.
- Let's put 2 pairs together and make groups of 4.
- When you're finished, find another pair and share what you came up with.

16 Group Work
그룹 활동하기

Teacher: Divide yourselves into groups of 3. Yeong-i, Jin-Yeong, and Myeong-ho, can you be a group?
Student: Okay.
Teacher: There are too many people in this group. Geum-ju, could you join that group?
Student: All right.

- Make 3 groups.
- Let's divide into 3 groups.
- I need you to split into 3 groups.
- I'm going to divide you into 3 groups.
- Get into your groups now, please.

- 3 people in a group.
- 3 in each group.
- Work in groups of 3.
- Get into groups of 3.
- Divide yourselves into groups of 3.
- Find 2 friends and make a group of 3.

- This is group work.
- Don't work alone—I want you to work in a group.
- Don't do this by yourself. Do this together.
- No one should be working alone on this.

- Yeong-i, Jin-Yeong, and Myeong-ho, can you be a group?
- Can the 3 of you make 1 group?
- Why don't the 3 of you work together?
- I want Mi-ran, Young-ho, and Su-mi to work in one group.

- There are too many people in this group.
- There should only be three people in each group.
- How many people should there be in a group?

◦ Let's work together.
◦ Come here.
◦ We need 5 people.

◦ We have too many people. Somebody needs to leave.
◦ We need 1 more person/2 more people in our group.

◦ Can you join our group?
◦ Do you want to work with us?

도움말

학생들이 교실영어에 어느 정도 익숙해 질 때까지 교사는 학생들과 관련된 표현을 주기적으로 복습하는 것이 좋습니다.

For example:
  Teacher: What if you have 3 people in your group, but you need 4 people. What can you say?
  Student: We need 1 more person.
  Teacher: What if you have 3 people in your group, but you need 4 people. What can you say?
  Student: We need 1 more person.
  Teacher: Yes, we need 1 more person in our group.

- Don't you have anyone to work with?
- Is everyone in a group?
- Don't you have a group?
- Are you by yourself?
- Do you need someone to work with?

- You can join that group.
- Geum-ju, could you join that group?
- Would one of you join the group over there?

◦ Can we have a group of 4?
◦ Is it okay if we have 4 people in our group?

> **도움말**
>
> 'group A'나 'group 1'과 같이 그룹 이름은 단수로 사용합니다.
>   incorrect: *Your group have 7 cards.
>   correct: Your group has 7 cards.

> **도움말**
>
> 학생들을 무작위로 나누는 일반적인 방법은 학생들의 수를 세어 나누거나, 각 학생에게 번호를 준 다음 같은 번호를 가지고 있는 학생들이 한 그룹을 이루도록 하는 것입니다.
>
> For example:
>   Teacher: Let's see. We should divide into 3 groups for this activity, so let's count off. Min-ho, could you start. You're number 1. Say it: '1'?
>   Student: 1.
>   Teacher: And then Geum-ju, what number are you?
>   Student: 2.

> Teacher: 2. Right. And you?
> Student: 3.
> Teacher: Yes. And we need 3 groups, so you start with number 1 again, and you're... what?
> Student: 2.
> Teacher: Uh-huh.
> Student: 3.
> Teacher: Okay. Now could the '1's come here by the windows? '2's go over by the door, and '3's meet in the back by the clock. '1's by the windows, '2's by the door, and '3's by the clock.

- Group 1, come here.
- Everyone who is in group 1, come here.
- Could I have all the '1's? Come here.

- This is group 1.
- You are group 1.
- We'll make all of you group 1.

- Choose a leader for your group.
- Each group should have a leader.
- Decide who is going to be the leader in your group.

- One person in each group should be the secretary.
- Pick one member of your group to write things down.
- Each group needs one person to keep track of the score.

- Each member of the group should take a different part.
- Everyone in the group has a special job.
- Please divide up the work in your group.

> **도움말**
>
> 'each member of the group' 구문을 사용할 때는 주의가 필요합니다. 다음을 참고하세요.
>
>   incorrect: *your group members/your members
>   correct: the members of your group

- I'll be the reporter.
- Can you be the secretary?

- I need a volunteer from each group to answer my question.
- Pick one person from your group to come to the front.
- Please choose a representative from each group.

17　Dividing into Teams
팀 나누기

Teacher: Get into two teams. You too, Hye-jin. Why don't you join Ju-won's team? Ju-won, what's your team's name?
Ju-won: We're 'The Tigers'.
Teacher: Hye-jin, you can be on 'The Tigers' team, okay?

- Get into two teams.
- Make two teams.
- Let me divide you into teams.

- You need to make a name for your team.
- What's the name of your team?
- What's your team's name?
- We're 'The Tigers'.

도움말

미국 스포츠 팀의 이름은 'The Chicago Bears', 'The L. A. Dodgers'와 같이 복수형을 사용하지만 단어 'team'은 단수로 사용됩니다. 그러므로 'Your team has three people.' 이나 'The Tigers have three people.'이라고 말하는 것이 맞습니다.

- Which team do you want to be on?
- Do you want to be on Cheol-hee's team?
- Why don't you join Ju-won's team?
- You can be on this team, okay?

◦ Can I be on that team?
◦ Which team am I on?

18. Asking for Volunteers
자원자 요청하기

Teacher: I need a volunteer. Who wants to volunteer? Raise your hand.
　　　　(한 학생이 손을 든다.)
Teacher: Great.

- I need a volunteer.
- Any volunteers?
- Who wants to do this?
- Can I have a volunteer?
- Who wants to do something special?

- Who wants to volunteer? Raise your hand.
- Raise your hand if you want to volunteer.
- I'll pick the first person to raise their hand.

- I need two volunteers.
- Could one pair come here and demonstrate once?
- Can I have some volunteers to come up do this?

- What! No volunteers?
- Come on. I know one of you wants to volunteer.
- If no one volunteers, I'll have to pick someone.

- Sun-sik has volunteered.
- Hee-jin is going to model this for us.
- Su-min will be our demonstrater.
- Thanks for volunteering.
- Thanks for being willing to do this.
- Let's give her a hand. (학생들이 박수를 친다.)

> **도움말**
>
> 자원하여 발표하는 것은 학생 입장에서는 대중 앞에서의 쑥스러움을 무릅쓰는 일이기 때문에 자원하는 학생들을 격려하고, 자신감을 심어주며, 발표를 마친 후에 감사를 표하는 것이 좋을 것입니다.

19 Movement, General Activity
동작, 일반 활동하기

> Teacher: Listen and do what I say. Stand up! Go over to the door. Turn around. Face the wall. Take three steps to the right. Freeze! Okay, go back to your chairs and sit down.

- Copy me.
- Go like this.
- Do what I do.
- Everybody, do this.

도움말

교사가 학생들에게 자신의 행동을 따라하라고 지시할 때 사용하는 표현입니다. 다음 내용에 유의할 필요가 있습니다.
  incorrect: *Follow my doing.
  awkward: *Follow my actions.
  correct: Do what I do.

- Listen and do what I say.
- Do what I tell you to do.
- Follow my instructions.
- Listen to the directions.

> **도움말**
>
> 'do what I say' 와 'do what I tell you to do' 라는 구문에 유의할 필요가 있습니다.
>
> incorrect: *Follow my saying.
> correct:　　Do what I say./Do what I tell you.
>
> 또한 'instructions'와 'directions'는 복수형이라는 사실에 유의할 필요가 있습니다.

- Stand up.
- Stand by your chairs.
- Could you all stand up?

- Sit down.
- Have a seat.
- Sit in your seats.
- Take your seats.

- Sit up straight.
- Take your feet off the desk.
- Put your feet on the floor.
- Don't get up.
- Stay in your seats.
- You don't have to stand up.

- Come here.
- Come to the front.
- Come and stand up here.
- Would you come over here?

- Go there.
- Go over to the door.
- Can you go stand by the door?

- Go out.
- Go out in the hallway.
- Would you go and stand in the hallway?

- Go out and we'll call you back in.
- Go out and come back in five minutes.
- Wait in the hallway until we call your name.

- Turn around.
- Turn all the way around.
- Face the other direction.

- Face the wall.
- Look at the wall.
- Turn your back to the class.
- Stand with your back to the class.
- Freeze!
- Don't move.
- Nobody move.
- Sit/stand still.
- Stay where you are.

- Walk to the right.
- Take three steps to the right.
- Walk around the circle to the right.

- Walk and sing at the same time.
- You need to sing while you're walking.
- Keep singing the song as you walk.

(그 외 동작에 관한 명령들)
- Fold your hands.
- Wave your hand.
- Wiggle your fingers.
- Blink.
- Stomp your feet.
- Shrug your shoulders.
- Hop on one/your left/your right foot.

- Now go and sit down again.
- Go back to your seats, please.
- Thank you, you can sit down again.
- Go back to your chairs and sit down.
- Back to your places.

- Raise your hands.
- Raise your hand if you know the answer.
- Put your hands up.

- Hands down.
- Put your hands down again.
- You can put your hands down now.
- You don't have to keep your hands up.

- Clap your hands.
- Let's clap (our hands) along with the song.
- Can you clap with the beat, like this?

> **도움말**
>
> 'let's' 또는 'let us'는 말하는 당사자를 포함하는 표현입니다.
>   incorrect: *Let's clap your hands.
>   correct: Let's clap our hands.

- Point to the right picture.
- Point out the right picture, please.
- Could you show us which picture is the right one?
- Point to the (picture of) the cheetah.

- Close your eyes.
- Eyes closed.
- No peeking!
- Everyone should have their eyes closed.

- If I say 'polar bear', point to the picture of the polar bear.
- When you hear 'I told you so', fold your arms.
- On the word 'help', stand up.
- If I tell the truth, clap your hands, but if I lie, stomp your feet.

> **도움말**
>
> 신체적인 반응을 요구하는 표현을 소개할 때는 교사가 먼저 답을 행동으로 보여 주고, 다음은 그룹으로서 학급 전체가, 마지막으로 개개인이 행동으로 답하도록 유도하는 것이 좋습니다.
> For example:

> Teacher: Point to the cheetah. (교사가 'cheetah'를 가리킨다.) Everyone! (교사가 전체 학급에게 제스처를 취한다.) Point to the cheetah. (교사가 'cheetah'의 그림을 다시 가리키고, 학생들이 흉내낸다.) Point to the rabbit. (교사가 'rabbit'를 가리키고, 학생들이 흉내낸다.) Point to the squirrel. (학생들이 'squirrel'을 가리킨다.) Se-nah, point to the cheetah. (한 학생이 'cheetah'를 가리킨다.)

- Come on!
- Hurry up!
- Do it quickly!
- Excuse me.
- Pardon me.
- Sorry, I need to get through.
- Could you let me through?

(다른 사람과 마주치며 이동할 때)
- You're in the way.
- You're blocking the way.
- There's not enough room with you standing there.
- Geum-ju can't get by.

- Line up.
- Get in line.
- Let's make a line.
- Line up by the door.

- Stay in line.
- Don't get out of line.
- Follow the leader.

20 Leaving the Classroom
교실 나가기

(잠시 교실을 떠날 때)
Excuse me for a moment.
I'll be back in a minute.
I'll be right back.

- Keep working while I'm gone.
- Just continue with what you're doing.
- Please go on with that exercise until I get back.

- I'm coming.
- I'll be right there.
- Wait a second.
- Just a minute.
- Hang on. (격식을 갖추지 않은 표현임)

21 Checking Comprehension
이해력 점검하기

Do you understand?
Are you with me?
Are you following me?
(Do you) get it? (informal) Got it.

- Do you know what I mean?
- Is that clear?
- Does that make sense?
- Is there anything you didn't understand?

○ I don't understand.
○ I don't get it.
○ Could you explain that again?

○ What?
○ What did you say?
○ Would you mind repeating that?
○ Could you say that again, please?

○ I'm okay.
○ I get it.

> **도움말**
>
> 교실에서 질문하는 것은 우수한 학생의 특징이지만 외국어로 질문하는 것을 꺼려하는 학생들이 종종 있습니다. 이런 경우 질문을 미리 가르쳐 주면 도움이 됩니다. 또한 용기를 내어 질문하는 학생들을 칭찬해 주는 것 또한 잊지 마시기 바랍니다.
>
> For example:
>   Student: I don't understand. Can you explain that again?
>   Teacher: Sure. Thanks for asking.

- Se-young, is this right?
- Is this right or wrong?
- Do you see any mistakes?
- Can you find any thing wrong with this sentence?

- What's the right answer?
- What should it be?
- How can you fix the mistake?
- Raise your hand if you know the answer.

- What do you think?
- How would you fix it?
- What would you say?

- Does anyone else have an idea?
- Are there any other answers?
- Did anyone come up with something else?

- Any questions?
- Are there any questions about this?
- Do you have any questions for me?
- Is there anything you want to ask me about?
- Would you like me to explain anything?

> **도움말**
>
> 'Is there anything you want to ask me about?'이라는 표현에 유의할 필요가 있습니다.
>
>   incorrect: *Is there anything you want to ask me?
>   correct: Is there anything you want to ask me about?

- If you have any questions, raise your hand.
- Raise your hand if you don't understand.
- If you need my help, just ask.
- If you get stuck, raise your hand, and I'll come over and help.

- Can you help me?
- I don't understand this.
- This is hard.

- What's the trouble? Tell me in Korean.
- What do you need help with?
- What are you having trouble with?

- Do you all know what to do?
- Does everyone know how to do this?
- Do you understand the directions?

- How do we do this?
- What are we supposed to do?

- Let me explain.
- Let me put it this way:
- I'll try to explain it another way.

- Does that answer your question?
- Does that make sense?
- Are you okay now?

- Do you know what all the words mean?
- Are there any words you're unfamiliar with?
- Can I help you with any words or phrases?
- Are there any words or phrases you don't understand?

- What does ... mean?
- What's a ...?

- Let's see if you got it.
- Let me check your comprehension.
- We'll check how well you understood.

- Put this in your own words.
- Tell me in your own words what happened.
- Can you paraphrase what happened?

- What is the story basically about?
- Could you summarize the story for us?
- Give me a brief summary of the what happened.
- Can you give me the main ideas of this paragraph?

22 Asking for Clarification
설명 요청하기

Teacher: Jung-bin, could you give us the answer to number one?
Jung-bin: The telegraph made it ...
Teacher: Pardon?
Jung-bin: The telegraph made it possible to communicate over long distances.

- What?
- Pardon?
- Excuse me?
- I'm sorry?
- I beg your pardon.

- What was that?
- I didn't hear you,
- Could you repeat that?

- You did what?
- You went where?
- You said what?

- Sorry. I don't understand.
- What do you mean?
- I'm not sure I know what you mean.

II. The Development of the Lesson

- Tell me in Korean.
- You can use Korean.
- Just say it in Korean.

23 Giving Feedback
피드백 제공하기

Student: Can I say 'Almost Koreans like Gim-chi'?
Teacher: No, that doesn't really work. You made a little mistake.
Student: What's wrong?
Teacher: The first word.
Student: Oh. Most Koreans like Gim-chi.
Teacher: Perfect.

- There's one mistake.
- You made a little mistake.
- See if you can fix the mistake.

24 Confirmation
확인하기

Okay.	
That's it.	All right.
Good.	Right.
Yes.	Fine.
Mm-hmm.	Uh-huh.

(작업의 질을 칭찬할 때)
- Good.
- That's good.
- Well done.
- Great.
- That was so good.
- Good job.
- You did a good job.
- Well done.

> **도움말**
>
> 'so good'이라고 표현할 때는 주의가 필요합니다. 'That was so good.'이라는 표현을 사용하는 것은 괜찮으나 'That was a so good speech.'는 틀린 표현입니다. 명사를 수식할 때 사용하는 올바른 표현은 'That was such a good speech.'입니다.
>
> incorrect: *That was a so good speech.
> correct: That was such a good speech.

(매우 잘된 일에 대하여)
- Excellent!
- Terrific!
- Wonderful!
- Fantastic!
- Very well done.
- I'm impressed!

> **도움말**
>
> incorrect: *very wonderful/very excellent/really terrific
> correct: wonderful/excellent/terrific

(한 개의 정확한 답에 대하여)
- Thank-you.
- That's right.
- That's correct.
- Yes, you're right.

- Perfect.
- Everything was right.
- You didn't make any mistakes.

- You understand.
- You know all of these expressions.
- You caught on quickly.
- I think you've studied hard.

- That's just what I was looking for.
- That's it.
- That's correct.
- That's exactly the point.
- Good. That's exactly what I wanted.
- Now that's just how I wanted you to do it.

○ Is this okay?
○ Is ... right?
○ Can I say ...?

- That's much better.
- You've improved a lot.

- Could be.
- In a way.
- It depends on the situation.
- In some situations that would work.

(학생이 놀라운 제안을 할 때)
- There are two possibilities.
- There is more than one right answer.
- Either answer works.
- Does anyone have a different answer?
- You could look at it that way.

- That's an interesting suggestion.
- I hadn't thought of it like that before.

- Not really.
- Not exactly. Try again.
- No that doesn't really work.
- Good guess, but I'm looking for something else.
- I'm afraid this is wrong.

> **도움말**
> 부정적인 표현은 사람보다는 실수에 초점을 두는 것이 바람직합니다. 예를 들어 'I'm afraid you're wrong.' 이라는 말은 무례한 표현처럼 들립니다. 실수에 초점을 두기 위해서는 'I'm afraid this is wrong.' 이라고 말하는 것이 더 좋습니다.

- You made a little mistake.
- That's not quite right.
- There was just a small mistake. Try again.

> **도움말**
> 학생에게 자기 수정의 기회를 주는 것이 좋습니다. 교사가 즉각적으로 수정하지 않는 방법을 사용하면 학생은 정답을 시도해보는 기회를 갖게 되고 성취감도 맛볼 수 있어 교육적으로 좋습니다.

- Where?
- What's wrong?

> **도움말**
> 실수임을 알게 하는 일반적인 방법은 질문에 억양을 넣어서 실수한 말을 반복하여 표현하는 것입니다.
> For example:
> Student: She went to home.
> Teacher: She went to home?
> Student: She went home.
> Teacher: Right.

- Let's listen to the sample dialogs. Are they like the ones you made?
- Is your dialog like the sample? Let's find out.
- Let's check the sample dialogs and compare them with the ones you made.

25 Leading to the Answer
정답 유도하기

Teacher: What's she doing tomorrow?
Student: Tomorrow she go swimming.
Teacher: Almost. Try again.
Student: Tomorrow she going swimming?
Teacher: You're on the right track.
Student: Mmm ...
Teacher: Take your time.
Student: Ahh ...
Teacher: Here's a hint: You need another word before 'going'.
Student: Oh. Tomorrow she is going swimming.
Teacher: That's it.

- Almost.
- You were almost right.
- You're on the right track.
- You almost have it.
- You're very close.
- You're almost there.

- Try again.
- Have another try.
- Okay. You can do it this time.

- You don't have to hurry.
- We have plenty of time.
- Take your time.

- Can you give us a hint?
- Would you like a hint?
- Do you want some help?
- Here's a hint.
- I'll give you a clue.

26 Encouragement
격려하기

Student: He caught a pish.
Teacher: A pish?
Student: A pish.
Teacher: Come on. You can do it. Concentrate.
Student: He caught a fish.
Teacher: That's better.
Student: A funny fish.
Teacher: Yes, you've got it.

- This is easy.
- This will be easy for you.
- You can do this. No problem.
- It's a piece of cake.

- Come on. You can do it.
- Don't give up.
- This is a little hard, but you can do it.
- I know this is tricky, but you can figure it out.

- Don't worry.
- You'll do fine.
- I'm sure you'll do okay.

- Don't worry about mistakes.
- If you make a mistake, that's okay.
- Don't be afraid of mistakes.
- A mistake won't kill you. (격식을 갖추지 않은 표현임)

◦ Thank-you.

- Think.
- Concentrate.
- Focus on what you're doing.

- That's better.
- That's more like it.
- You've improved.
- You've made progress.
- You're getting better at it all the time.

(작업 중인 학생에게)
- That's it.
- Okay, that's the idea.
- Yes, you've got it.
- You have the idea now.

- You're doing very well.
- You're really working hard.
- I'm very pleased with how you're doing.

27 Evaluation
평가하기

Teacher: Here is your test. The grammar was very good, but the dictation was a little hard for you, wasn't it?
Student: Yes.

- I'm going to evaluate this on Friday.
- We're going to have a spelling check on Friday.
- Be ready for an evaluation on Friday.

- While you're speaking, focus on using past tense verbs.
- In the interview, I'll be listening for correct stress.
- As you're working on this, remember that I'll be evaluating your pronunciation.

- You have good pronunciation.
- You spelled everything right.
- The grammar was very good.

◦ Thank you.

- You need to work on your pronunciation.
- The spelling dictation was a little hard for you, wasn't it?
- You need a little more practice with grammar don't you?

II. The Development of the Lesson

- How can I make it better?
- How can I improve my spelling?
- What can I do?

* That wasn't very good.
* You can do better than that.
* Come on, try a little harder.

- Okay. I will.
- Let me try again.
- Can I try again?

28 Giving Opinions
의견 제시하기

Teacher: I can't stand the smell of smoke.
Student: Me neither.
Teacher: I think smoking should be illegal. What do you think?
Student: Me too.
Teacher: Is there anyone who doesn't agree, or do you all think that smoking should be illegal?
Student: I disagree.
Teacher: How come?

- Was it [the movie] good?
- Was it a good book?
- Did you like it?
- How did you like it?
- Did you find it interesting?
- What did you think of *AVATAR*?

○ It was great.
○ I loved it.
○ It was kind of boring.
○ I thought it was stupid.

- What part did you like the most?
- What part was the best?
- What was the best part?

II. The Development of the Lesson

- My favorite part was when ...

* What do you think (of ...)?
* What's your opinion (of ...)?
* How do you feel about this?

* Do you like playing computer games?
* Don't you like D.D.R.?
* You don't like romance novels, do you?

> **도움말**
>
> 'likes'나 'dislikes'에 대하여 말할 때 명사를 복수형으로 만들어야 합니다.
>
>   incorrect: *Do you like playing computer game?
>   correct: Do you like playing computer games?

- I like science-fiction most.
- I like to be alone sometimes.
- There's nothing I like more than soccer.

* I don't like waiting in line.
* I hate it when people lie.
* I can't stand the smell of smoke.
* I think cheating is wrong.

- Me too.
- Me neither.
- Same here. (격식을 갖추지 않은 표현임)

> **도움말**
>
> 'Me too.'와 'Me neither.'는 동의를 표현할 때 사용합니다. 전자는 긍정적인 말에 동의할 때 사용되며, 후자는 부정적인 말에 동의할 때 사용됩니다.

- Do you agree (with him/her/me)?
- Do you think so too?
- Am I right?

- Do we all agree?
- Is there anyone who doesn't agree?
- Does anyone want to disagree?
- Do you all think that ...?
- How come?
- Why (do you like it)?
- Why not?
- Why do you like D.D.R.?
- Why do you think the book is interesting?
- Can you tell me why you said so?

○ That's a good idea.
○ That's a good point.
○ I couldn't agree more.
○ That's just what I was thinking.

○ I don't think so.
○ I don't agree.
○ I can't accept that.

도움말

'like'는 직접목적어를 필요로 하는 동사입니다.

    incorrect: *Why do you like?

    correct: Why do you like it?/Why do you like computer games?

29 Showing Preference
선호하는 것 제시하기

> Teacher: If you had to choose one, which would you choose: the cat or the dog?
> Student: The cat.
> Teacher: The cat! No way! Really? Do you all like cats better than dogs? Let's take a vote. If you like the cat better than the dog, raise your hand.

- What do you want?
- Do you want to do this in class now or do it as homework?
- Would you like to review this again or are you ready to go on to something new?
- Would you rather be the secretary or the reporter?

  ○ I want to do it now.
  ○ I'd like to be the secretary.

- What did you like better?
- Do you like this better than the other one?
- If you had to choose one, which would you choose?

- Pick one.
- Choose a topic.
- What would you like to work on?
- Is there something in particular you are interested in?

II. The Development of the Lesson | 141

- You can decide.
- It's your decision.
- It's up to you.

- I don't mind either way.
- Either way is fine with me.
- It doesn't make any difference to me.
- It's all the same to me.

- Let's take a vote.
- We'll put it to a vote.
- We'll let the majority decide.

- Who likes A better?
- If you like A better, raise your hand.
- Everyone who likes A better, raise your hand.

- Most people like A.
- It looks like a majority of you like A better.
- Okay. 12 of you like A better and only 3 of you like B.

> **도움말**
>
> 학생의 손을 들게 하는 여론 조사는 모든 학생들에게 신체적으로 의견을 표현할 수 있도록 기회를 제공하는 것입니다. 일단 학생들이 스스로 자신의 의견을 밝히고, 그 다음으로 구두로도 자신의 견해를 표현하도록 하면 의사소통적 구연 연습에 도움이 됩니다.
>
> For example:
>   Teacher: If you like A better, raise your hand.
>   (학생들이 손을 든다.)
>   Teacher: Jung-min, you didn't raise your hand. Why don't you like A? ... Su-yeon, you raised your hand. Why do you like A?

30 Explaining and Giving Examples
설명 및 예시하기

> Teacher: Here's what you need to do. Turn these into passive sentences. Make sure you use the past participle of the verb.
> Student: Is this right?
> Teacher: Yes, that's fine.

- How do you do this?
- What are we supposed to do?
- This is how you do it.
- Here's what you need to do.
- Let me explain how to do it.
- Do it this way.
- I'd like you to do it like this.

- Let me give you an example.
- Here is an example.
- Let me show you how to do it.
- Let's do one together.

> **도움말**
>
> 'for example'이라는 표현은 영어 구어보다는 문어에서 더 보편적으로 사용됩니다. 'for example'을 짧은 단어 목록을 소개하는 데 사용하지는 않습니다. 그러므로 'Do you like sports, for example, baseball, softball, soccer?'라는 말은 부자연스럽습니다. 짧은 단어 목록을 소개할 때는 'like' (casual) 나 'such as' (moderately formal)를 사용하는 것이 더 좋습니다. 따라서 'Do you like classic movies like *Gone with the Wind* or *The Wizard of OZ*?'는 자연스러운 표현입니다.

- Is this right?
- Could you do it like this?
- Is this what you want?

(교사가 답을 모를 때)
- I'm not sure.
- I have no idea.
- I really don't know what to say.
- I have nothing to say right now.
- I'm not sure what to tell you.

- Try to do it like we did last time.
- Do it the same way we did last time.
- Remember how we did it last time? Do it like that.

- You have to
- Make sure you ...
- Remember to ...
- Don't forget to ...

II. The Development of the Lesson

31 Class Control and Discipline
수업 통제하기 및 훈육하기

> Teacher: Stop passing notes.
> Student: Sorry.
> Teacher: I don't want to see you doing that again.

- Sit down, please.
- Sit still, please.
- Sit down and listen to me.

- Quiet, please.
- Su-young, be quiet, please.
- Stop talking.

32 Establishing Rules
규칙 설정하기

These are the rules.
This class has a set of rules.
We have some rules in this class.

- Remember the rules.
- Always follow the rules.
- Never break the rules.
- Good students always keep the rules.

- No cheating.
- You should never cheat.
- Cheating is not allowed.
- Cheating is against the rules.

> **도움말**
>
> 종종 학교 수업 훈육이나 경고에 관련된 표현들을 사용할 때 동명사형을 활용합니다. 예를 들면, 'No cheating.', 'Cheating is not allowed.', 그리고 'Cheating is against the rules.' 등이 있습니다. 'To cheat is not allowed.'는 어색한 표현입니다.

- Do your best.
- You should always do your best.
- One rule is that all students should do their best.

(학생들이 하는 일을 즉시 중단해야 할 때)
- No, don't.
- Don't do that.
- That's enough.
- Hey! Stop!
- Stop it right now!
- Stop it this minute!

- Never do that again.
- Don't do ever that again.
- Don't let it happen again.
- This is the last time.
- I don't want to see you doing that again.

◦ Sorry.
◦ I'm sorry. I won't do it again.

- I'm angry.
- I'm very upset.
- I'm very unhappy about this.
- This really makes me mad.

- Stop passing notes.
- Why are you passing notes?
- What are you passing notes for?
- You shouldn't be passing notes.

- That's childish.
- You're being silly.
- Is that a mature thing to do?

- Be quiet.
- Don't talk.
- Stop talking.

- Settle down.
- Calm down.
- Not so much noise please.

- What's going on here?
- What on earth are you doing?
- What do you think you're doing?

- Don't cheat or you'll fail.
- If you cheat, you'll automatically get an F.
- If I catch you cheating, I'll take your test away.

33 Getting Attention
주의 집중시키기

Teacher: Okay! Look at me. I'm waiting until I have everyone's full attention. Yoon-mi, turn around and face me. Please concentrate. You need to understand this.

- Okay!
- All right!
- Now!
- Everyone!
- Class!
- Look!
- Listen!

- Look up here.
- Look at me.
- Could I have your eyes?
- May I have your attention please?
- I'm waiting until I have everyone's full attention.

> **도움말**
>
> 영어 수업에서는 특히 학생들의 집중을 방해하지 않도록 주의해야 합니다. 주변 소음은 한국어 강의를 들을 때보다 영어 강의를 들을 때 더 방해를 받는다는 것을 기억하십시오. 모국어로 말할 때 보다 외국어를 말 할 때에 두뇌신경학적으로 집중 에너지를 더 많이 사용하기 때문입니다.

- Stop and look at me.
- Stop where you are and listen for a minute.
- Could you stop what you're doing and look up here?
- I hate to stop you, but I need to explain something.

- Face the front.
- Turn this way.
- Turn around and face me.

- Stop day dreaming.
- Focus on what we're doing.
- Please concentrate.

- This is important.
- This is something you need to know.
- Listen. You need to understand this.

34 Warning
경고하기

Teacher: Be careful!
Student: Ow!
Teacher: Are you okay?
Student: Yeah, I'm okay.
Teacher: Is it bleeding? Let me see.
Student: Yes, a little.
Teacher: You better go to the nurse.

(어떤 물체가 학생을 칠 때)
- Be careful!
- Look out!

(공중에 방해물이 있을 때)
- Watch out!
- Duck!

(바닥에 방해물이 있을 때)
- Watch your step.
- Don't trip.
- Watch out for the chord/step.
- Stay away from that.
- You better not go there.

- Ouch!
- Ow!
- Oh!

(학생이 우울해 보일 때)
- What's wrong?

(사고가 발생했을 때)
- What's the matter?
- What happened?
- Are you okay?
- Did you get hurt?
- Does your leg hurt?

- Yeah, I'm okay.
- I was just surprised.
- My leg (hurts)!

- Don't worry.
- It's all right.
- It'll be okay.

- Is it bleeding?
- Did it break the skin?
- Do you need a bandage?

- You should see the nurse.
- I think you should see the nurse.
- You'd better go to the nurse.
- Do you want to go to the nurse's room?
- I suggest you go and see a doctor.

- You should really be more careful.
- Try to be more careful next time.
- Next time watch where you're going.

◦ Okay.
◦ I will.

35 Giving Permission
허락하기

Student: Can I go get my book?
Teacher: Okay. But I want you back here in five minutes.
Student: Thanks.

- Can I try?
- May I have a turn?
- May I go now?
- May I go to the bathroom?
- Can I get a drink of water?
- Can I have some more?
- Can I turn in the homework on Friday?
- Can I go get my notebook?
- May I see you next Monday?

> **도움말**
>
> 학생들이 교사에게 무엇인가 질문하고 싶어 하는 상황에서 교사가 유용한 표현을 알려주면, 학생들이 즉각적으로 활용할 수 있는 기회가 되기 때문에 학습 효과가 높습니다.
>
>   Student: (학생이 자신의 notebook을 가지고 싶어하는 제스처를 취한다.)
>   Teacher: Can I go get my notebook?
>   Student: Can I go ...?
>   Teacher: Get my notebook.
>   Student: Get my notebook.
>   Teacher: Now the whole thing: can I ...?
>   Student: Can I go get my notebook?
>   Teacher: Sure.

- Okay.
- Sure.
- Sure, you can.
- Why not?
- No problem.
- Of course, you may.
- That's fine with me.

- Fine. Go quickly.
- All right. But do it quickly.
- Go ahead. But I want you back here in five minutes.
- Okay. Just this once.

- You may use a dictionary.
- I don't mind if you turn it in on Friday.
- It's okay to take some more.

- If you need to, you can say it in Korean.

○ Thanks.

- Could you wait?
- Could you do it later?
- Do you have to do it now?

- No. Not now.
- No. I need you here for this.
- No. I don't want you to miss this.

- Please don't.
- No, don't do that.
- I'm afraid not.
- I'd rather you didn't
- I don't think that's a good idea.
- Sorry, I can't let you do that.

○ Please, can I?
○ Just this once?

36 Apologizing
사과하기

Teacher: Oops! Did I step on your foot? Sorry about that.
Student: That's okay.

- Sorry.
- Sorry about that.
- Excuse me.
- Sorry for doing that.
- I'm sorry. I didn't mean to do that.

도움말

'sorry for + 동명사'의 구조를 사용할 때는 주의가 필요합니다.
   incorrect: *Sorry for my doing that.
   correct: Sorry for doing that.

- Oops.
- Oh, I made a mistake.
- Sorry, I didn't notice that.
- I must have over-looked that.
- I must be getting absent-minded.

(심각한 실수에 대한 공식적인 사과)
- It's all my fault.
- I owe you an apology.
- I can't tell you how sorry I am.
- I really shouldn't have done that.

(사과에 대한 반응)
- That's okay.
- That's all right.
- Don't worry about it.
- Never mind.
- No problem.
- It really doesn't matter at all.
- It's all right this time.

- I'm terribly sorry, but it wasn't my fault.
- I feel bad about it, but I really had no choice.
- I understand how you feel, but there's nothing I can do about it.

37 Offering Help
도움주기

Teacher: That looks heavy. Could I give you a hand?
Student: That would be great.

- Can I help you?
- Can I give you a hand?
- What can I do to help?

(도움을 수락할 때)
- That's nice of you.
- Sure, thanks for offering.
- Oh would you? Thanks.
- That would be great.
- How nice of you.
- You're so kind.

(도움을 거절할 때)
- I'm all right. Thanks.
- That's okay. I've got it.
- You don't have to.

38 Thanking
감사하기

Teacher: I appreciate your help.
Student: Anytime.

- Thank you.
- Thanks a lot.
- Thank you very much.

- Thanks for helping out.
- I appreciate your help.
- It was nice of you to help me.
- You've been very helpful.
- Thank you for (cleaning up).

도움말

'thanks for + 동명사' 구조를 사용할 때는 주의가 필요합니다. 'thanks for (gerund)'와 'thank you for your (noun).' 의 다음 예를 참고하세요.

   incorrect: *Thank you for your helping.
   correct: Thank you for helping.

II. The Development of the Lesson

- You're welcome.
- My pleasure.
- It's my pleasure.
- Sure.
- Anytime.
- Don't mention it.
- If you need me, just ask.

39 Giving
나누기

Teacher: I brought some candy today.
Student: Can I have one?
Teacher: Go ahead. Take one. There should be one for each student.

- These are for you.
- I have something for you.
- Would you like one?

○ Yes, please.
○ Yes. Thank-you.
○ No, thank-you. (I'd rather have some apples.)
○ No thanks. (I've had enough.)
○ That's all right.

○ Can I have one?
○ May I try one?
○ Are these for us?

- Help yourself.
- Go ahead. Help yourself.
- Go ahead. Take one.

- You may each have one.
- Take one each.
- I've brought one for each of you.
- There should be one for each student.

- Do you want some more cake?
- Could I get you another one?
- Do you have enough, or would you like some more?

- Would you like something to drink?
- Can I get you anything to drink?
- What would you like to drink?

(다른 사람에게 물건을 건넬 때)
- Here.
- Here you are.
- There you go.
- It's a present. Go ahead, open it. I hope you like it.

40 Congratulating/Well Wishing
축하/축복하기

Student: We won every game this season.
Teacher: Congratulations!
Student: We have another game tonight.
Teacher: Good luck.

- Good luck!
- I'm rooting for you.
- I hope you make it.
- I hope everything goes well.

(졸업, 수상 등 어떤 일을 성취했을 때)
- Congratulations!
- I'm glad to hear that!
- You must be proud!
- Good for you!
- What an accomplishment!

도움말

    incorrect: *Congratulation.
    correct: Congratulations.

- That's too bad.
- That's a pity.
- Sorry to hear that.
- I'm sorry to hear the bad news.
- I know how it feels.

- Cheer up.
- Don't take it so hard.
- Look on the bright side.

- Better luck next time.
- I'm sure you'll do better next time.
- Oh well. You can always try again.

PART III

Language Practice
언어 연습

PART III

Language Practice
언어 연습

1. **Spelling** 철자법에 대하여 이야기하기
2. **Pronunciation** 발음에 대하여 이야기하기
3. **Vocabulary** 단어에 대하여 이야기하기
4. **Grammar** 문법에 대하여 이야기하기
5. **Listening** 듣기
6. **Storytelling** 이야기 말하기
7. **Asking for Clarity and Volume** 명확성 및 소리 크기 요청하기
8. **Brainstorming** 브레인스토밍하기
9. **Dialogue** 대화하기
10. **Show and Tell** 보여주며 말하기
11. **Acting Out/Skit** 연극/촌극하기
12. **Discussion** 토론하기
13. **Reading** 읽기
14. **Writing** 쓰기
15. **Handwriting** 손으로 쓰기
16. **Doing Exercises** 연습활동하기
17. **Games** 게임하기
18. **Songs and Chants** 노래와 챈트하기
19. **Drawing** 그림 그리기

1 Spelling
철자법에 대하여 이야기하기

Teacher: Can you spell 'knife' for me?
Student: n-i-f
Teacher: Oops. Try again.
Student: n-i ... n-i ...
Teacher: You need another letter at the beginning.
Student: What letter does it start with?
Teacher: K. Knife begins with a silent k.

- Spell 'orange'.
- How do you spell 'orange'?
- Can you spell 'orange' for me?
- How is 'orange' spelled?

도움말

'Spell orange.'와 'Can you spell orange for me?'라는 표현은 이미 학생들이 단어를 알고 있는 경우 확인하기 위해서 질문할 때의 표현이므로, 'How do you spell orange?'가 더 일반적인 유형입니다. 학생들은 'How do you (verb)?' 구문을 다양한 상황에서 유용하게 사용할 수 있을 것입니다.

How do you spell this?
How do you pronounce this?
How do you do this exercise?

III. Language Practice

- Is this spelled right?
- Can you find the spelling mistake?
- There is a spelling mistake. Can you find it?
- Can anyone fix the spelling?

- Check your spelling.
- I think you have a spelling mistake.
- It looks like there's a spelling mistake.

> **도움말**
>
> 'This is the wrong spelling.'라는 문장은 잘못된 표현입니다. 'This is spelled wrong.'이라는 표현은 괜찮지만 좀 더 정중하게 말할 때는 'Check your spelling.'이라고 표현하는 것이 좋습니다.

- What letter does it start with?
- What's the first letter?
- What letter comes first.

> **도움말**
>
> 'letter'와 'alphabet'이라는 단어에 관하여 살펴보면, 글자(letter)는 하나의 알파벳을 가지지만 알파벳은 26개의 글자로 이루어집니다. 알파벳은 복수형이 불가하지만 글자는 복수형이 가능합니다.

- It starts with a 'k'.
- The first letter is 'k'.
- 'Knife' begins with a silent 'k'.

> **도움말**
>
> 관사와 알파벳을 사용할 때 주의가 필요합니다. 모음 중에서 첫소리가 자음으로 발음되어 관사 'a'를 사용하는 경우가 있으며, 자음 중에서도 첫소리가 모음으로 발음되어 'an'을 사용해야 하는 경우도 있습니다.
>
> an: A, E, F, H, I, L, M, N, O, R, S, X
> a: B, C, D, G, J, K, P, Q, T, U, V, W, Y, Z

- Spell it 'o-u'.
- First 'o' and then 'u'.
- The 'o' and the 'u' are backwards.
- Switch the 'o' and the 'u' around. 'R' not 'i'.
- Make this an 'r'.
- Change this 'l' into an 'r'.
- This should be an 'r,' not an 'l'.

- What letter is missing?
- What's the missing letter?
- You need another letter at the beginning.
- What letter do you/we need here?

- You need an 'e'.
- Put an 'e' at the end.
- You just need to add an 'e' to the end.

- You need another 'o'.
- You have to have one more 'o'.
- It's spelled with two 'o's.
- Double 'o'.

- You need 't-w-o' here. Not 't-o'.
- Not that kind of 'to'. The number 2.
- That's the preposition 'to'. How do you spell the number 2?

- Write it as one word.
- Write it all together.
- Don't leave a space.
- Don't write it as two separate words.

- You have to put a hyphen here.
- This word is hyphenated.
- Put a hyphen between 'clear' and 'cut'.

- Use a big 'n'.
- You need a capital 'n'.

- Remember to capitalize 'New York'.
- Write 'New York' with a capital N.
- 'New York' starts with a capital letter.

- Use all small letters.
- You don't need to use big letters.
- You don't need to capitalize that word.

- All the letters are in the wrong order. Can you put them in the right order?
- This is a word, but the letters are mixed up. Can you figure out the word?
- This is an anagram. See if you can spell a different word with the letters.

2 Pronunciation
발음에 대하여 이야기하기

> Teacher: Listen. Don't speak. Watch my lips. 'Did the suspect take a right or a left?' Now listen and repeat after me. 'Did the suspect ...'
> Students: 'Did the suspect ...'
> Teacher: 'Take a right or a left?'
> Students: 'Take a right or a left?'
> Teacher: Listen to my intonation: 'take a right or a left?'

- Let's work on pronunciation.
- Now it's time to practice pronunciation.
- How about a little pronunciation practice?

도움말

'pronunciation'은 불가산명사입니다.
    incorrect: *Let's work on some pronunciations.
    correct: Let's work on some pronunciation.

- Listen.
- Listen carefully.
- Just listen this time.
- Listen. Don't speak.
- Listen very carefully this time.

- Listen to me.
- Listen to Myung-ho.

- Watch carefully.
- Watch and listen.
- Watch my lips.
- Pay attention to how my mouth moves.
- Read my lips. What am I saying?

> **도움말**
>
> 추측 게임이란 교사가 소리 없이 입모양으로 단어를 말하면 학생들은 교사의 입모양만 보고 단어를 맞추는 게임입니다. 이 활동은 학생들로 하여금 구강 움직임에 집중할 수 있도록 도와줍니다.

- Listen to the intonation.
- Notice when the pitch goes up and down.
- When does my voice go up and when does it go down?

- Listen and repeat.
- Listen and repeat after me/the recording.
- Everyone, repeat after me, 'park'.
- Repeat/Say it again, please.

- Okay. Now you try.
- Say it like I did.
- Try to pronounce it how I did.

- Can you make it a little smoother?
- It sounds too choppy.
- Connect the words.

- Now try to smooth it out.

- Where is the stress in this word?
- The second syllable is stronger.
- Stress the second syllable.
- You need more stress on the second syllable.

- This way: 'Brazil'.
- Say it like this: Brazil.
- Listen to how I say it: Brazil.

- Make the 'l' with the tip of your tongue.
- Your tongue needs to be just behind your teeth for the 'l'.
- The tip of the tongue needs to touch the alveolar ridge.
- Don't stick your tongue through your teeth.

- The back of your tongue needs to go up when you say 'r'.
- Your tongue needs curl up when you say 'r'.
- The front of your tongue shouldn't be too high when you say 'r'.
- Don't let the tip of your tongue touch the roof of your mouth.
- Put your tongue between your teeth for the 'th'.
- When you say 'th,' you need to have your tongue between your teeth.
- Your tongue needs to be between your teeth when you say 'th'.

- You need to touch your lips together for 'b' and 'p'.
- Your lips need to touch when you say, 'beep'
- If your lips don't close, you're not saying it correctly.

- Don't close your mouth when you make the 'v' sound.
- Your lips shouldn't touch when you're saying 'victory'.
- When you make an 'f' or a 'v,' you need to touch your bottom lip to your top teeth.

- 'Wood'. Not 'ood'.
- When you make a 'w', your lips need to start out small and then get bigger.
- Your lips have to be tighter for the 'w' than for the 'oo'.
- You have to pucker your lips for the 'w'.

- Not 'tom'. 'Top'.
- You need a little air after the 'p'.
- Open your lips after the 'p'.
- You have to release the 'p' at the end of 'top'.

- Don't add 'ee' to the end of 'orange'.
- Say 'orange' and stop. Don't say 'orangee'.
- Don't add a vowel sound to the end of the word.

- You write these words the same, but you say them differently.
- These words are spelled the same, but pronounced differently.
- The spelling is the same but the pronunciation is different.

3 Vocabulary
단어에 대하여 이야기하기

> Teacher: First I want to teach you a few words. Let's see how many you already know. What do you call this in English?
> Student: Slide.
> Teacher: Is there another word that means the same thing?
> Student: Slip.

- First I want to teach you a few words.
- I'd like to introduce some new vocabulary.
- I think these words will help you later on.

도움말

어휘(vocabulary)는 단어들(words)의 집합입니다. 그래서 'Someone who knows a lot of English words has a large vocabulary.'라는 표현이 가능합니다.

- Do you know all of these words?
- Are there any words here that are unfamiliar?
- Look over this list of words and tell me if there are any you don't understand.

- Maybe some of you already know these.
- Let's see how many you already know.
- I want to check whether you know what these words mean.

- What's this?
- What kind of clothing is this?
- Who knows what this is?
- What do you call this in English?
- What's the English word for this?
- Can you guess what the English word is?

- What does this word mean?
- When do you use the word '_____'?
- When do you think you would say '_____'?

- This means...
- This means the same as...
- This means something like....

- What part of speech is it?
- Is it a noun or a verb?
- How is it used in this sentence?

- What's another word for 'bounce'.
- What's a synonym for 'bounce'?
- Give me a synonym for 'bounce'.

- What's a word that means the same thing?
- What's another word for it?
- Can you find another word with the same meaning?
- Who can give me a synonym for this word?

- What does 'cool' mean here?
- How is 'cool' used here?
- What does it mean in this context?

- What's the opposite of 'beautiful?'
- What means the opposite?
- What means 'not beautiful?'

- What's one word for 'become better'?
- How can you express 'become better' in one word?
- What's a shorter way of saying 'become better'?

- Can you make 'beauty' into an adjective?
- What's the adjective form of 'beauty'?
- Can you think of an adjective that has to do with 'beauty'?

- If you mean 'chicken,' don't say 'kitchen'.
- Try not to confuse 'kitchen' and 'chicken'.
- Don't mix up 'chicken' and 'kitchen'.

- I'll say the meaning and you guess the word.
- I'll give you the definition you give me the word.
- I'll describe a word and then you guess what I'm talking about.

- It begins with 'c'.
- It starts with a 'c'.
- The first letter is 'c'.

- It rhymes with 'bat'.
- It sounds like 'bat'.
- It ends with 'at'.

> **도움말**
>
> 교사는 단어의 철자 또는 소리와 관련지어 힌트를 주어도 좋습니다.
> For example:
>   Teacher: I'll give you the definition you give me the word. This is a kind of animal that eats mice. It begins with 'c', it rhymes with bat, and it has three letters. What is it?

4 Grammar
문법에 대하여 이야기하기

Student: Book where?
Teacher: Where is ...
Student: My book.
Teacher: Start from the beginning and say the whole sentence. Start with 'where is...'
Student: Where is my book?
Teacher: Perfect.

- You can use 'is' plus 'i-n-g' for things that happen in the future.
- You could use 'is' and an 'i-n-g' verb to make a sentence about something in the future.
- 'Is' and 'i-n-g' show that something is happening right now or in the future.

- Is this sentence correct?
- Is this sentence right?
- Can you fix that sentence?
- Is there anything wrong with that sentence?
- Is it okay the way it is, or is there something wrong?

> **도움말**
>
> incorrect: *a right sentence/a wrong sentence
> correct: a correct sentence
> an incorrect sentence:
>   Is this sentence right?
>   Is there something wrong with this sentence?

- This sentence isn't right.
- This sentence has a mistake.
- This sentence is incorrect.
- There is something wrong with this sentence.

- Singular or plural?
- Should this be singular or plural?
- Do you want singular or plural here?

- What verb tense do we need here?
- What kind of verb goes here?
- This is happening right now, so what tense should I use?
- Do we need past tense here? Then what tense do we need?
- Use 'is' and 'ing'.
- Use present continuous.
- How do I make this present continuous?
- Tell me how to say it.

- The article goes before the adjective.
- Say the article first, then the adjective.
- Where do you put the article?
- Where should the article go?

III. Language Practice | 183

- You need a noun here.
- You need to use a number word.
- Answer the question with a feeling word.

- Is that the right word order?
- Are the words in the right order?
- Is that the order the words should go in?

- Check the word order.
- The words are in the wrong order.
- Which word should come first?
- You have the right words, but they're in the wrong place.

- One word is missing.
- You're missing a word.
- What word is missing?
- Fill in the blank: I went to BLANK post office.

- You forgot the article.
- You left the article out.
- You need 'a', 'an', or 'the'.

- Are you sure you want 'the' here?
- You don't need an article here.
- Never put 'the' before someone's name.

- Which preposition comes after concentrate?
- What preposition does concentrate take?
- Do you 'concentrate **about** something' or do you 'concentrate **on** something?'

- When do you use 'say' and when do you use 'tell'?
- Do you remember the rule for using 'say' and 'tell'?
- Do you 'say a story' or do you 'tell a story'?

- This isn't a complete sentence.
- This doesn't have a subject.
- This is a fragment.

- Don't start a new sentence.
- You can make this all one sentence.
- You don't need a period here.
- This can all be one sentence.

- Okay. Now say the whole sentence.
- Start from the beginning and say the whole sentence.
- Use a complete sentence.

- Start with 'Where is...'
- This time start with 'Where'.
- The question word goes at the beginning.
- Put the question word at the beginning.

- What else could you say?
- How else could you say it?
- Can anyone say it another way?
- Try to put it in other words.
- Could you phrase it slightly differently?

- Say, '...'
- You can say it like this: '...'
- The English expression for that is '...'

- People usually say...
- A native speaker would say...
- The grammar is okay, but It's more common to say...

5 Listening
듣기

Teacher: You're going to hear a conversation. Listen for the main idea—don't worry about understanding every word. When we're finished listening, I want you to tell me why Judy is angry. Okay. Here it is. (교사가 녹음 내용을 들려준다.)
Teacher: What were they talking about?
Student: Money.
Teacher: Do you remember why Judy was angry? No? Do you want me to play it again?
Student: Yes.
Teacher: Okay. I'm going to ask you how Judy replies to Susan, so listen carefully.

- We're going to listen to a conversation.
- I'm going to play a conversation for you.
- I'd like you to listen to a conversation.

- You're going to hear people talking at a grocery store.
- This is a conversation between a customer and a cashier at a grocery store.
- This is something you might hear at a grocery store.

- What will the man say?
- What do you think the man will say?
- What words do you think you'll hear?

III. Language Practice | 187

- Can you guess what they'll say?

- Let's listen to the dialog now. Ready?
- Now we'll listen to the conversation.
- I'll play the conversation now.

- Listen for the main idea.
- Don't worry about understanding every word.
- Don't try to catch every word.
- Just try to figure out basically what it's about.

- While you're listening, could you answer these questions?
- As you hear the conversation, try to figure out why Judy is angry.
- When we're finished listening I want you to tell me why Judy is angry.
- Keep these questions in mind while you're listening.
- Remember, we will discuss these questions after you're finished watching.

- As we listen, fill in the blanks.
- Listen for the missing words.
- You need to listen for the words that are missing.

- When you hear one of these words, raise your hand.
- Everytime you hear a preposition, raise your hand.
- When you hear the answer, I want you raise your hand.

- How many people are talking?
- How many different voices do you hear?
- This time try to figure out how many people are in the conversation.

- I'll play it twice.
- I'm going to play it two times, so don't worry if you don't catch everything the first time.
- You're going to hear it twice. Just listen for the main ideas this time.

- I'll pause after each line.
- I'll stop the audio file after each person speaks.
- I'll stop the recording and give you time to write.

- Close your books and listen to the recording.
- Please listen with your books closed.
- Keep one finger on this page and close your book while we listen to the recording.

- Let me ask you some questions about what you just heard.
- I have a few questions for you about the recording.
- Are you ready to answer some questions?

- Okay, so what did they say?
- What were they talking about?
- How much do you remember?

- Did you hear what they are eating for lunch?
- Did you figure out what they are eating for lunch?
- Do you remember what they are eating for lunch?

- Should we listen to it again?
- Do you need to hear it again, or are you okay?
- Do you want me to play it again?

- Let's listen again.
- I think we need to hear it again.
- We'll listen to it one more time.
- Let's listen again for the answer to number 2.

> **도움말**
>
> 'I think we need to hear it again.' 이라는 문장에서는 직접목적어가 반드시 있어야 합니다.
>
>   incorrect: *I think we need to hear again.
>   correct: I think we need to hear it again.

- Who wants to listen again?
- Does anybody want to hear it again?
- If you want to hear it again, raise your hand.

- This time tell me who says, 'Gotcha'.
- Try to remember exactly what Judy says.
- This time tell me exactly what phrase Judy uses.
- I'm going to ask you how Judy replies to Susan.

- Listen and repeat.
- Repeat after the recording.
- Everyone say it together after the recording.
- Say it exactly like the woman on the tape. Imitate her voice.

- Please listen and write the words you hear.
- We're going to do some dictation.
- I'd like you to write down what I say.

> **도움말**
> Dictation은 쓰는 행위가 아니라 말하는 행위입니다. 교사가 단어를 말할 때(dictates) 학생들은 그 단어를 받아 쓰는 것입니다.

6 Storytelling
이야기 말하기

> Teacher: Come over here by me. I'm going to tell you a story. I'm going to tell you the story of 'Goldilocks and the Three Bears'. The story goes like this. Once upon a time there were three bears: a Pappa Bear, a Momma Bear, and a little Baby Bear. One day the Bear Family...

- Come over here by me.
- Sit where you can see.
- Why don't you come a little closer so you can see?

- I'm going to tell you a story.
- I have story to tell you today.
- Are you ready to hear a story?

- I'm going to tell you the story of 'Goldilocks and the Three Bears.'
- Do you know 'Goldilocks and the Three Bears'?
- The story is called 'Goldilocks and the Three Bears'.

- The story is about a girl named Goldilocks.
- In the story there is a girl named Goldilocks.
- Your going to hear about a girl named Goldilocks.

- Listen to the story.
- Listen very carefully.
- Get ready to listen.

- Okay. Let's begin.
- Here's the story:
- The story goes like this:

> **도움말**
>
> 교사가 동화 읽어주기를 끝낼 때는 'And that's the story of *Goldilocks and the Three Bears.*'와 같이 동화 제목을 반복해 주는 것이 일반적입니다.

- Act out the story while I tell it.
- I'll tell the story again. Act like you are Goldilocks.
- I want you to pretend that you are Goldilocks while you hear the story again.

7 Asking for Clarity and Volume
명확성 및 소리 크기 요청하기

> Student: I like ...
> Teacher: I'm having trouble hearing you. Could you say it a little louder.
> Student: I like comic books and video games.

- Louder, please.
- Speak up.
- Could you say it a little louder?
- I'm having trouble hearing you.
- You're a little too soft. Please say it louder this time.

- Say it clearly, please.
- Could you speak more clearly?
- Slow down and articulate.
- Try to make each sound clear.

8 Brainstorming
브레인스토밍하기

> Teacher: Let's do some brainstorming. What can you do in winter?
> Student: Go skiing.
> Teacher: Good. What else?
> Student: Wear warm clothes.
> Teacher: Good now brainstorm with a partner. What else can you do in winter? Write down as many ideas as you can.

- Let's do some brainstorming.
- Let's brainstorm about things you can do in winter.
- Try to think of as many things as possible that you can do in winter.

- You can say anything.
- Anything is okay.
- It's okay to say silly things.

- Say as many words as possible.
- The important thing is to say a lot.
- Write down as many ideas as you can.
- We are going for quantity, not quality.

- What else?
- What else can you think of?
- Can you think of anything else?
- See if you can add a few more items to the list.

9 Dialogue
대화하기

> Teacher: Let's make up a conversation. Let's say you're invited to a movie and you don't want to go. What could you say?
> Student: No.
> Teacher: Okay. But what if your friend invites you to the movie. Remember you don't want to hurt your friend's feelings. What could you say?
> Student: I don't have time.
> Teacher: Okay. Changmin and I will do it together. I'll call you up and ask you to go to a really boring movie. What movie is really boring?
> Student: *Two Thousand One.*
> Teacher: Then I ask you to see *Two Thousand One*. Ready? Ring! (Answer the phone. Say, Hello.)
> Student: Hello.
> Teacher: Do you want to go see *Two Thousand One*?

- Let's move on to a dialogue.
- Now we're going to practice a conversation.
- I'd like you to practice a dialogue.

도움말

'conversation'과 'dialogue'의 사용에 주의할 필요가 있습니다
  practice a conversation
  have a conversation/a dialogue

> practice a dialogue
> do a dialogue
> (incorrect: *Let's converse.)

- Let's make up a conversation.
- Let's write a dialogue together.
- I'd like you to help me make up a conversation.

- Let's say that you're invited to a movie but you don't want to go.
- Let's pretend that you want to stay home tonight but your friend asks you to a party.
- What if your friend asks you to a party but you want to stay home?
- If you were invited to a party but you didn't want to go, what would you do?

- When can you say this?
- In what situation would you use this expression?
- Can you think of a situation when you could use this expression?

- What could you say?
- What do you think you would do?
- What question could I ask?
- How would you respond in that situation?

- You're going to hear some people making excuses.
- Listen for how these people give excuses.
- Let's find out how these people give excuses.

III. Language Practice | 197

- Let me do it for you first.
- I'll demonstrate.
- I'll show you how to do it.
- I want you to do something like this.

- Watch how I do it.
- Listen carefully to how I do it.
- Watch me this time.

- Chang-min and I will do it first.
- Min-su, let's do it once together.
- Joon-ho, let's demonstrate for the rest of the class.
- Ji-hye is our expert. We'll show you how to do it.

- Yong-hee and Han-su, will you do it for the rest of the class?
- Eun-sook and Hee-ja, could you come to the front and demonstrate?
- Chan-mi and Dong-hee, will the two of you show us how to do it?

- Let's practice the conversation.
- I think we're ready to do the conversation ourselves.
- Now let's try it on our own.

- Everyone together this time, and then we'll do it again in pairs.
- Let's practice once altogether, and then you can try it in pairs.
- Let's read the dialogue in unison, and then we'll break up into pairs.

- Okay, why don't you try it with a friend?

- You work in pairs. One of you should be Judy and one should be Beth.
- Do the conversation again with a partner.

- Look down at your book and read the sentence. Then look up at your partner and speak.
- Read the sentence. Memorize it. Then look up and say it to your partner.
- Look at your partner, not your paper.
- Look at your partners when you're talking to them.
- You can't talk while you're looking at your book.

- First do it with your books, and then try it without looking.
- This time you may look at the words, next time with the books closed.
- Okay, close your books. This time try to remember it without looking.

- You can change the dialogue. Use the words at the bottom of the page.
- This time personalize it. Give information about you.
- Now use your own names. Make it about you.

- Make up your own conversation like this one.
- Make your own dialogue. Use this one as a model.
- Why don't you continue the conversation on your own?

- The dialogue should go like this.
- You need to include these things in the dialogue.
- Remember to thank your partner and then end the conversation.

(워크쉬트나 워크카드를 가리키며)
- I'm going to give you cue cards.
- The card says what you have to do.
- The card tells you who you are.
- If the card says TAXI DRIVER, act like a taxi driver.

- Let's act out this dialogue.
- Now we'll act the conversation out.
- Let's role play the situation.
- If you were A before, now you're B. If you were B, now you're A. Do it again.
- Now switch roles and do it again.
- Trade parts and practice the dialogue again.

- Could you act this out for us?
- Why don't you do it once in front of the class.
- Come out to the front and show everyone else what you did.

- Byung-chul and Hae-in, would you come here and do it for us?
- Would you mind performing your dialogue for the class?
- Are you two ready to show the rest of us?

10 Show and Tell
보여주며 말하기

Teacher: I brought something to show you. This is something really special. Who knows what you call this? No one? It's a dream catcher. Can you guess what it does?
Student: Does it catch dreams?
Teacher: Exactly. These are made by Native Americans. If you hang it over your bed at night, all of the bad dreams are supposed to get caught in the spider web.

- What's this?
- What is it?
- What do you call this?
- Who knows what you call this?
- Do you know what this is called in English?
- What's the English word for this?

- This is very important.
- This is something really special.
- This is one of a kind.
- To me, it's the best in the world.

- This means a lot to me.
- This is very important to me.
- This brings back a lot of memories for me.

- I thought you would enjoy it.
- As soon as I saw this, I wanted to bring it to class.
- When I found this, I thought, 'I should bring this to English class'.

- I got this ... in Alaska.
- This is from a street market in India.
- These are made by Native Americans.

- I've had this ... for twenty years.
- I got it ten years ago/when I was in high school?
- This is thirty years old.
- This is older than I am.
- I've been saving this for a long time.

- A friend of mine gave this to me.
- I got this from a friend.
- I inherited this from my grandmother.

- Have you ever used one of these before?
- What do you think it's used for?
- What do you do with it?
- When would you use it?
- Can you guess what it does?

- You use this when you...
- This is for ...ing.
- You can use this to...

- I like this because ...
- The reason I like this is that ...
- This is special to me because ...

- I have been keeping this.
- I have been saving this to show you.
- I want to save this forever.

- Pass it around the room.
- You can each have a look.
- Take a look at it, and then hand it on to the next person.

11 Acting Out/Skit
연극/촌극하기

Teacher:	Could you act out this conversation? Let's see... first we need to divide up roles. Hyun-chul, who do you want to be?
Hyun-chul:	I want to be Jack.
Teacher:	Fine. And Yoon-ju, what about you?*
Yoon-ju:	I don't know.
Teacher:	Okay. Then you can read Judy.

> **도움말**
>
> 'What about you?'는 대화 중 이전의 질문이나 진술에 대하여 묻는 것입니다. 이러한 경우 'Who do you want to be?'나 'What about you?'는 그 자체로는 의미가 없기 때문에 대화를 시작할 수는 없는 표현입니다.

- Pretend you're a monkey.
- Act like a cowboy.
- Walk like a penguin.

- Mime juggling.
- Act like you're playing basketball.
- Pretend you're playing the piano.

- Let's do a role play.
- I'd like you to roleplay this situation.
- Each of you choose a character and then act out this situation.

> **도움말**
>
> 'do a role play'라는 표현의 사용에 주의할 필요가 있습니다.
> incorrect: *Play a role play.
> correct: Do a role play.

- Let's put on a skit.
- We're going to perform a scene.
- Could you act out this conversation?

- First we need to decide who plays each part.
- Let's divide up the roles.
- Could you each choose a character?
- Pick the character you would like to play.
- Who do you want to be?

- Do you want to play Jack? (Okay. /No, not really.)
- Who wants to be Jack? (I do./Not me.)
- Does anyone want to play Jack? (I do./Not me.)
- Can I have a volunteer to play Jack? (Me./Not me.)
- Raise your hand if you want to play Jack.

∘ I want to be Jack.
∘ Can I read Jack?

- You be Judy.
- You're Judy.
- You play the woman.
- You can read the woman's part.

- Use movement this time.
- How does your character move? What is he doing?
- Is he reading a newspaper? Then read a newspaper.
- This time let's stand up and do it with movement.

- Act like a taxi driver.
- Can you mime driving a taxi?
- Pretend that you are driving a taxi.

- Face the audience.
- Turn toward the audience.
- Don't turn your back on the audience.

- Read it with feeling!
- Don't speak in a monotone.
- Remember, Judy is angry.

- Say it to Hyun-chul.
- Look at the other actor when you say your line.
- Look at the person you're talking to.
- Look at Yoon-ju when you're talking to her.
- Let's practice without the script.
- Shall we do it for memory this time?
- This time try to do it without looking at your script.

- You can be the prompter.
- Read along silently, and if the actor gets stuck, you give him a hint.
- Follow along in your script, and if the actor can't remember his lines, you read the first few words.

- This is the dress rehearsal, so let's work hard.
- It's our final practice, so do your best.
- This is our last chance to practice, so let's make it wonderful.

- **Break a leg!** (연기를 시작하려고 하는 연기자들을 격려하는 전통적인 표현입니다.)

12　Discussion
토론하기

Teacher: Today we're going to have a discussion on home economics, so I'd like you to divide into groups of 5. Each group should put their chairs in a circle. Good. Now each group is going to be a family and you have to decide how to spend your money. How much money are you going to spend on clothes? How much on food? How much on recreation? Look at the 'Home Economics' handout for ideas. Now 1 person from each group should be the secretary and write everything down, okay? Good. Then go ahead.

- We're going to have some time for discussion today.
- Today we're going to have a discussion on home economics.
- Later on today, I'd like you to discuss this issue in small groups.

- Pick a topic.
- Which one would you like to discuss?
- What topic do you want to talk about?

- Have you thought of a discussion topic?
- Do you know what you want to talk about?

◦ We want 'The Environment'.
◦ We want to talk about 'The Environment'.

- ◦ We don't have a topic yet.
- ◦ We don't agree.

- The purpose of the discussion is to...
- You have to decide how to...
- Your group has to figure out what to do.
- You need to come to a consensus in your group.

- Divide into groups.
- You can split up into discussion groups now.
- Go sit with your groups.
- Let's divide into groups for the discussion.

- This is the topic.
- I'd like you to talk about ...
- You need to discuss ....

- Talk about this in your group.
- Talk to your group about this.
- Discuss the problem in your group.

- Each group should discuss a different topic.
- I'll assign each group a different topic.
- You in this group take topic A. You over there should take topic B.

- This is the process.
- Here's what you should do first...
- I want you to go through these steps.

- Each group needs a leader/secretary/researcher.
- You need to pick a group leader.
- Choose a secretary for your group.
- Who's the researcher in your group?
- Have you chosen a secretary?

- The secretary should take notes.
- One person from each group should be the secretary and write everything down.
- The secretary should report to the class what you did.
- Secretaries, get ready to share your notes with the class.

- Here are the rules for the discussion.
- You need to follow a few rules as you do this.
- I'm going to give you a few rules as you discuss this.
- Remember to...

- Listen to the person who's speaking.
- Everyone should pay attention to the speaker.
- Don't interrupt when other people are talking.
- Be quiet and listen to the person who's speaking.

- Don't shout.
- You don't need to talk so loudly.
- Please keep the volume down.

- One person from each group should report to the class.
- One person should tell the class what you talked about.
- Could I have a representative from each group tell us what you did?

- You have 10 minutes.
- Try to finish in 10 minutes.
- I'll give you 10 minutes to come to a conclusion.

- Following the rules is part of your grade.
- I will grade you on how well you follow the rules.
- I'm going to look for how well you follow the guidelines as you do the project.

◦ We're finished. What do we do now?

- If your group finishes early, you can move on to the next topic.
- When your group is finished, please go on to the next issue.
- Are you finished? Good. Then you can discuss the next situation.

- Please move your seats together.
- Each group should put their chairs in a circle.
- Move your chairs together with the other members of your group.

- Make a circle.
- Let's put all the chairs in a big circle.
- Let's combine the groups to make one big group.

- Let's divide the chairs into three groups.
- Can we make three circles?
- Let's move the chairs into three circles.

- It's time to finish up.
- Try to finish what you're talking about.
- We have to move on, so get ready to stop.

- Are you almost finished?
- Is your group done?
- Have you discussed everything?
- Have you covered all the topics?

○ Yes, we're finished.
○ No, we're not done yet.
○ We need a little more time.
○ Can we have a little more time?

- So, what did your group decide?
- Would you tell us what your group did?
- Please read what your group came up with.
- Could you read us what you talked about?

- Show us your results.
- Show us what you made.
- Show us how you organized this.
- Could we see what you've done?

- Could you report for your group?
- Myung-hee, would you tell us what your group did?
- Can you read your summary for us?
- What did your group come up with?

- Pay attention to the other groups.
- Listen to what the other groups have to say.
- I might ask you questions about what the other groups are saying, so pay attention.

- I'm going to record your discussion so you can listen to it later.
- I'd like you to make a recording of your discussion.
- Would you please record your discussion?

- Please listen to your discussion.
- I want you to listen to the recording of your discussion.
- I'd like you to hear what you sound like.

- Let's vote on it.
- Let's take a vote.
- How many of you are in favor/against?
- Raise your hand if you like A better.
- This is a democracy, so we'll put it to a vote.

- Let's hear the results.
- What did you decide?
- What was the vote?
- How many of you were for and how many of you were against?

- I'm very pleased with your work.
- You followed the instructions well.
- You did everything I wanted you to do.
- Good work/Good job.

- Next time you do this, I'd like you to make sure everyone talks.
- You did fine, but next time try to cover all of the topics.
- Good work, but when we do this again, concentrate on following all of the steps.

- I wrote down some of your mistakes while you were talking.
- I've taken a few notes about common mistakes.
- I'd like to point out a few mistakes that people were making during the discussion.
- Let's practice this again.
- Let's go over this together.
- I'd like you to talk about this again. This time think about how you're saying it.

13 Reading
읽기

Teacher: Let's do some reading. Open your books to page 25. Look at the picture. What do you think the story is going to be about?

Student: A space station?

Teacher: Right. We are going to read about the space station Mir, and you are going to learn about what life is like in outer space. Would any of you like to live in outer space? (몇 명의 학생들이 손을 든다.) Some of you. Well, let's read the story. We'll take turns. Everyone reads one paragraph. Tae-ho, would you start? Read out loud, please.

> **도움말**
> 읽기 활동에 필요한 단어들에는 passage, story, article, essay, poem, novel, character, main character, point-of-view, plot 등이 있습니다.

- It's time to go on to reading.
- Let's do some reading.
- I have a story for you today.
- Now we're going to read a story.

- Can you guess what the story is about?
- What do you think the story is going to be about?
- Before you start reading, guess what happens in the story. Do you have any ideas?

- Let's read the story.
- You may begin reading.
- You can start reading now.

- Read it silently.
- Don't read it aloud.
- I'd like you to read the article to yourselves.
- Would you to read this quietly to yourselves?

- We're going to read about ...
- This story is about ...
- The article tells us about ...

- Read aloud.
- I want you to read this aloud.
- Don't read silently. I'd like you to read out loud.

> **도움말**
>
> 'Read loudly.'는 큰 소리로 읽으라는 의미지만, 'Read aloud.'는 다른 사람들이 여러분이 읽는 소리를 들을 수 있도록 보통 성량으로 읽으라는 의미입니다.

- Read one paragraph each.
- We'll take turns. Everyone reads one paragraph.
- Let's go around the room, paragraph by paragraph, starting with Tae-ho.

◦ Where do I start?

- Start reading at the beginning of the first paragraph.
- Would you read the first paragraph for us?
- Do you see where the paragraph begins? Start there.

- You start where Tae-ho left off.
- Begin with the next sentence.
- Would you start the next sentence for us?

◦ Should I stop/keep going?

- Keep reading.
- Keep going with the next sentence.
- Keep reading until I stop you.

- Stop there.
- That's good.
- That's all. Thank-you.

- Let's read all together.
- I want everyone to read at the same time. Ready?
- Shall we all read aloud together?

- Try to finish reading the article in 15 minutes.
- I'll give you 15 minutes to finish reading.
- You have 15 minutes to read the article.

- Read it aloud in your groups.
- Take turns reading in your groups.
- Go around your circle. Everyone should read a sentence.

- If you don't know the word, sound it out.
- Read it slowly. Think about the letters.
- What sound does 'p-h' make?

- Circle the words you don't know.
- If you don't know a word, circle it.
- When you see a word you don't know, put a circle around it.

- Scan for the proper nouns.
- Quickly find all the words that start with capital letters.
- Don't read the whole article. Just look for the answers to these questions.

- Underline the main idea.
- Find the topic sentence.
- Underline the sentence that shows what the whole paragraph is about.

- Listen and read silently.
- I'll play the CD, and you try to follow the words in your books.
- Why don't you follow along in your books as I play the audio file?

- Whenever I stop, you fill in the next word.
- When I stop reading, everyone says the next word.
- I'll start then you continue reading where I leave off.

- Who are the characters in the story?
- What are the character's names?
- Who are the people in the story?

> **도움말**
>
> 토론하거나 이야기를 요약할 때에는 일반적으로 현재 시제를 사용하여 말합니다.

- Where does the story take place?
- What's the location of the story?
- Where do the characters live?

- How does the story begin?
- What's the first thing that happens?
- What happens at the beginning of the story?

- What's the conflict in the story?
- What's the problem?
- Why can't the main character get what she wants?

- What do you think happens next?
- Can you guess what happens next?
- What should the characters do next?
- How would you finish the story?

- What was the main idea?
- What was the article basically about?
- Can you summarize the passage in one sentence?

- Why does the author think that?
- Can you find any evidence to support that idea?
- What reasons does the author give to support the main point?

- Read the passage and answer the questions.
- When you're finished reading, answer the questions.
- Answer the questions after the story.

- What is the story about? Use just one or two sentences.
- Write a short summary of the story.
- Can you summarize the story?

- Was anything new or interesting for you?
- Did you learn anything new from the passage?
- Was there anything you didn't know before?
- What did you learn while you were reading the story?

- What paragraph talks about this?
- Try to find the paragraph that talks about this.
- Where in the article would you find out about this?

14 Writing
쓰기

> Teacher: We're going to do some writing, so take out a pen or a pencil. I'd like you to each write a paragraph about the ideal friend. First, make a list. Write down as many ideas as you can about friendship. What words could you use to describe a good friend?

- We're going to do some writing.
- I'd like you to write a few sentences for me.
- Would you each write a story?
- I'm going to give you a chance to do some writing.

- Take out a pen or a pencil.
- Get something to write with.
- You need something to write with.

- Fill in the blanks.
- Write the missing words in the blanks.
- You need to write the missing words in the blanks.

- Rewrite this part using the expression in parentheses.
- Substitute ... for this part of the sentence.
- You need to rewrite the last part of each sentence.

III. Language Practice

- Can we use another expression here?
- Can we put this another way?
- Is this the only way to write it or can you think of another way?

- Write a few sentences about friendship.
- I'd like you each to write a paragraph about the ideal friend.
- Take out a piece of paper and jot down a few ideas about what a good friend should be like.

- Write your own ending for the story.
- Finish the story on your own.
- Imagine what happens next. Write about what you think the characters will do.

- Take notes.
- Don't write everything down — just the most important words.
- Write down the words you want to remember.

- Pick a topic.
- Choose a subject that you are interested in.
- Think of something you would like to write about.

- Make a list of your ideas.
- Put your ideas in a list.
- Write down as many ideas as you can.
- Write down all of the things you think of.
- Make a list. Write down everything you can think of that's connected with this idea.

- Let's start with some free-writing.
- I'll give you ten minutes. Just write whatever comes to mind.
- Write as much as you can without stopping. It doesn't have to be perfect.

- I want you to write a paragraph like this one.
- This paragraph is similar to what I want you to write.
- You can use this paragraph as a model.

- What are the main points of this paragraph?
- Let's pick out the main points.
- Now we'll outline the main ideas.

- Plan your paragraphs.
- Arrange your points.
- Make an outline.

- Leave a margin on both sides.
- Indent each paragraph.
- Leave a space at the bottom of the page.
- Capitalize all of the important words in the title.

- Don't make the title too big.
- Use the same letter size for your title as the rest of your paper.

- Center your title.
- The title should be at the top of the page in the center.
- Put the title in the middle of the page at the top.

- Don't underline your own title.
- Put your own title in quotation marks/brackets/arrows.

- The date goes month-day-year.
- Write the month first, then the day, then the year.
- Remember to put the date month-day-year.

- Write it in pencil/in pen/in ink.
- Use a pencil
- Do it in pencil.
- I'd like this in pencil.

15　Handwriting
손으로 쓰기

Teacher: This is too messy. I can't read this. Watch me. Make the 8 like this, okay?
Student: Okay.

- Write it neatly.
- Write it so that I can read it.
- Make sure I can read your handwriting.
- Be careful with your hand writing.

- This is too messy.
- I can't read this.
- Your handwriting is illegible.

- The loop on the nine goes this way.
- The loop goes over here.
- The loop on the nine needs to go to the left.
- The loop on the 'p' needs to go to the right.
- Make the 8 with one line, not two circles. Start at the top.
- Watch me. Make the 8 like this, okay? Okay.
- Can you make the 8 with one line, like this?

- The 'g' needs a hook on the bottom.
- The 'y' needs to sit on the line and it has a tail that hangs down.
- The tail goes below the line.

- Please print.
- Write in cursive.
- Use all capitals.
- Write in block letters.

16 Doing Exercises
연습활동하기

Teacher: Let's do some exercises from your books. Could you turn to the exercises on page 41? We'll do the first one together and then you can try the rest on your own. Min-uk, can you read the question for us?
Student: (reading) When did the Berlin Wall come down?
Teacher: Who knows the answer? Look at the time line.
Student: 1989?
Teacher: Right. Now make that a complete sentence. Start with 'The Berlin Wall ...'
Student: The Berlin Wall fell in 1989.
Teacher: Do the other questions just like that. Make sure you use past tense verbs. Do the first ten questions, okay?

- Let's do some exercises from your books.
- Now we'll work on some of the problems in your books.
- Could you turn to the exercises on page 41?

- Do this in your workbooks/on a separate sheet of paper.
- Use your own paper for this.
- Write your answers on your own paper.
- You need a piece of paper for this activity.

- Do exercise A part 1.
- Start with exercise A part 1.
- I want you to do exercise A.
- Could you do the first part of exercise A now?

- First we'll practice orally, and then you can write it down.
- Let's talk through it once before you do it in your books.
- We'll do the first one together, and then you can try it on your own.

- Let's go on to the next exercise.
- I think we can move on to the next problem..
- You can do the next exercise too.

- Follow the example.
- Do it like the example.
- Look at the example and do it the same way.

- Fill in the blanks.
- Write the missing words.
- Choose one of the words at the top of the page and write it in the blank.
- Complete the sentences with the words in the box at the top of the page.

- Use the hints provided.
- You can use the words in the box.
- Take the words in parentheses. Put them in the right form and use them in the sentence.

- Complete the chart.
- Fill in the missing information.
- Add the missing information to the right column.

- Circle the best answer.
- Put a circle around the correct answer.
- Find the best answer and circle it.

- Check the right answer.
- Put a checkmark in the right box.
- Write a checkmark next to the right answer.
- Write a checkmark in the appropriate column.
- Underline the stressed syllable.
- Draw a line under the accented syllable.

- Match the words and meanings.
- Draw a line from the words to the definitions.
- Put the number of the definition next to each word.

- Answer true or false.
- This is a true-false exercise.
- You have to circle true or false.
- You need to figure out whether the sentence is true or false.

- Put these in order.
- Number the pictures in order from 1 to 10.
- Write which one comes first, which one comes second, and so on.
- Put the answers in the correct order.

- Use the hints to make complete sentences.
- Please rewrite these notes in complete sentences.
- Expand the notes into complete sentences.

- Make a sentence out of the following words.
- Use these words to make a sentence.
- Put these words in the right order.

- Cross out the word that doesn't belong.
- Draw a line through the word that doesn't belong.
- If you see a word that doesn't belong, cross it out.

- Use these words in a sentence.
- Put these words into a sentence.
- Write a sentence that shows the meaning of each word.

- Put the sentences into past tense.
- Make all of these sentences past tense.
- Change all the verbs into past tense.
- Rewrite the sentences using the correct form of the verb.
- Rewrite the passage. Use the correct form of the verbs.
- Add 'er' or 'est' to the adjectives.
- Add the right endings.
- Put the correct ending on each of the adjectives.

- Substitute 'didn't' for 'did not'.
- Replace the long form with the contraction.
- Use the contraction wherever you see the long form.

- Change the sentences. Use these phrases.
- Make sentences just like that one, but this time use these expressions.
- Do you see the phrases underneath? Substitute those for the underlined phrase.

- Answer the questions on page 12.
- Do all of the questions on page 12.
- Do numbers 1 though 10 on page 12.

- Do you understand what to do?
- Do you know what you have to do?
- Get it? (격식을 갖추지 않은 표현임)

  ◦ Got it.

- Don't start yet.
- Wait until I say you can start.
- Don't start until I tell you to.

- Go ahead.
- You can start now.
- You may begin.

- Raise your hand when you're finished.
- If you're done, raise your hand.
- When you have done all of the exercises, raise your hand.

- Check your answers with a partner.
- Compare your answers with the person sitting next to you.
- Find a partner and see if you got the same answers.

- Let's check our answers.
- Let's go over this together.
- It's time to go over the answers.

- What's the answer for number 1?
- How did you answer number 1?
- What did you get for the first problem?

- And then ...
- And number 2 ...
- And the next one ...

> **도움말**
>
> 어떤 연습문제들에는 'numbers'가 매겨져 있고, 어떤 연습문제들에는 'letters'가 표시되어 있습니다. 'letters'로 표시된 연습문제를 가리킬 때에는 'Number B.'라고 하지 말고, 'Letter B.'라고 불러야 합니다.
>
>   incorrect: *number B
>   correct: letter B

17 Games
게임하기

Teacher: Let's play a game. I'm thinking of an animal. Guess what animal I'm thinking of.
Student: Is it a pig?
Teacher: No. Guess again.
Student: Is it a mouse?
Teacher: No. You can ask me yes/no questions about the animal. Ask me questions like 'Is it big?' or 'Is it dangerous?'
Student: Is it big?
Teacher: No.
Student: Is it yellow?
Teacher: No. Do you give up?

- Let's play a game.
- I think it's time for a game.
- Now we're going to play a game.

- Get into two teams.
- Whose turn is it?

  ◦ It's mine/ours.
  ◦ It's Min-su's.

- Now, it's your turn.
- It's Se-young's turn now.

- Two points for team C.

- This team has won.

> **도움말**
>
> Eenie meenie minie moe
> Catch a tiger by the toe.
> If he roars, let him go.
> Eenie meenie minie moe
>
> 'Eenie, meenie'는 그룹에서 한 가지를 선택하는 일반적인 어린이들의 라임 배우기 활동입니다. 박자에 맞추어 하나를 가리키는데, 해당 학생이 라임 끝에 가리키는 것이 대명사 'it'이 됩니다.

- The name of the game is 'Twenty Questions'.
- This game is called 'Charades'.
- We are going to play 'Speed'.

> **도움말**
>
> 'game'은 관사와 함께 사용하지만, 경기 이름을 말할 때는 관사를 사용하지 않습니다.
>
> incorrect: *We are going to play speed game.
> correct: We are going to play 'Speed'.
>   We are going to play the speed game.

- Would you go out for a minute?
- Min-ho, could you leave the room for a few minutes?
- Min-ho, would you go out in the hallway while we do something secret?
- Go out and we'll call you back in when we're ready.

> **도움말**
>
> 추측하기 게임을 진행할 때는 학생 중 한 명을 교실에서 나가게 하고, 교실 안에 남아 있는 학생들은 추측하는 학생이 답을 추론할 수 있도록 비밀로 해줍니다.

- I'm thinking of an animal.
- Guess what it is.
- Guess what's missing.
- Can you guess what I'm thinking of?
- Try to figure out what I'm thinking of.

- Think of an animal.
- You all have to write down the name of an animal.
- Each team needs to come up with an animal.

- Now this is your secret.
- Keep it a secret.
- Don't tell him/her.
- Don't give the answer away.
- Make him/her guess.

- You have to guess which one it is.
- Everyone else has to guess what animal it is.
- The other team has to guess the name of the animal.
- They have to guess what animal you picked.

- Ask me yes or no questions.
- You have to ask yes and no questions.
- I can only answer 'yes' and 'no'.
- Ask questions like this: 'Is it big? Is it dangerous?'

- Guess what's in my bag.
- I have three things in my bag. Guess what they are.
- Try to guess what I'm thinking of.

- (교사가 동작을 묘사하면서) What am I doing?
- Guess what I'm doing.
- I'm going to mime something. See if you can figure out what I'm doing.

- (한 학생에게) Pick a word. Mime it. (학급에게) What is she doing?
- (학급에게) One person acts out the word. Everyone else guesses what the word is.
- (학급에게) I'll show you a picture. You act it out, and the rest of you guess what the picture is.
- (한 학생에게) Will you mime one of these expressions? Then we'll guess what you're doing.

- What's missing?
- What's gone?
- What was there last time that isn't there now?

- You have three guesses.
- I'll give you three guesses.
- If you don't get it in three guesses, then I win.

◦ I know!
◦ I've got it! It's a ...

> **도움말**
>
> 많은 게임에서 참여자들이 정답을 찾는데 서로 도움을 줍니다. 추측하는 학생이 정답에 근접할수록 비슷하다고(warmer) 말해 줄 것이고, 정답에서 멀어질수록 답과 거리가 멀다고(colder) 말해줍니다.

- You're freezing.
- You're very cold.
- Colder.
- Cold.
- Warmer.
- You're getting warmer.
- Hot!
- You're boiling!
- You're burning up!

- Don't say the answer!
- Don't give away the answer — let them guess!
- You're not supposed to talk while you're miming.
- Do you give up?
- Do you want me to tell you the answer?
- Are you ready to give up, or do you want to keep guessing?

III. Language Practice

- I give up.
- No, I want to keep playing.

- Whoever guesses first is the winner.
- The first person to say the correct answer wins.
- If you get it right, you win!

- Let's do 'Rock, Scissors, Paper' to see who starts.
- Could the team captains come here and do 'Rock, Scissors, Paper'?
- Shall we flip a coin to see who goes first?
- We'll have a coin toss to see which team gets the first turn.

- Heads or tails?
- What would you like: heads or tails?
- Your call: heads or tails?

- Ready. Set. Go! (for starting a race)
- Ready... Go!
- 1, 2, 3, Go!
- On your mark. Get set. Go!

- Roll the die/dice.
- Roll and then move that number of spaces.
- Roll for points. You get the number of points that are on the dice.

- Whoever guesses first gets a point.
- If you get it right, you get a point.
- One point each time you get the right answer.

- Let's play to ten.
- When you get ten points, you win.
- The first team that has ten points wins.

- One point for the women.
- The women get one point.
- That's one more point for women's team.

- You have nine points!
- The women have nine points!
- The score is nine to seven!

- You're almost there.
- You only need one more point to win.
- Maybe you can win this turn.

- Come on. You can catch up.
- You're not that far behind.
- Maybe you can catch up this turn.

- If you speak Korean, you lose a point.
- If I hear you speak Korean, I'll take away a point.
- If someone on your team speaks Korean, you automatically lose a point.

○ He spoke Korean!

- Whose point was that?
- Who answered first?
- Who got that first?

- It's my/our point.
- We got it first.

- Count up your points.
- How many points did you get?
- What was your final score?

- Who won?
- Who got the most points?
- Do we have a winner?

- You win!
- You came in first!
- The 'Tigers' are the winners!

> **도움말**
>
> 'You are the winner.'라는 문장이 틀린 표현은 아니지만 'You won.' 이라는 표현이 좀 더 보편적입니다.

- It was very close.
- You almost had it.
- You were a close second.

- It's a tie.
- You have the same number of points.
- You both won.
- We have to break the tie.
- We have to find a winner.
- I think we need to go into overtime.

- Congratulations!
- Nice job!
- Good work!
- Let's give them/him/her a hand!

> **도움말**
>
> 'a hand' 가 박수의 의미로 사용될 때는 항상 단수로 사용합니다.
>   incorrect: *Let's give them hands.
>   correct: Let's give them a hand.

- Did you enjoy the game?
- Was it fun?

18 Songs and Chants
노래와 챈트하기

> Teacher: Why don't we sing something. Let's sing 'Nobody's Home'. Do you that one?
> Student: No.
> Teacher: We haven't sung it before, so it may be new for most of you. Don't sing this time. Just listen. We'll sing in a minute.
> Teacher: I think we're ready to try singing it. What to you think? Are you ready to sing it or do you want to hear it one more time first.
> Student: Ready.
> Teacher: All right. Let's sing. Ready ... and ...

- Let's sing.
- Now, we'll sing a song.
- Let's all sing a song.
- I feel like doing a chant.
- Why don't we sing something?

> **도움말**
>
> 'Let's sing a song.'이라고 하는 것이 맞는 표현이지만, 'Let's sing.'이 더 자연스럽습니다. 'sing' 동사와는 달리 'do' 동사는 직접목적어를 취하기 때문에 'Let's do.' 문장은 비문이며, 'Let's do a chant.'는 정문입니다.

- What would you like to sing?
- What's your favorite song?
- Do you have a favorite chant?
- Bu-hung, would you like to pick a song for us?

- Do you know this song?
- Do you recognize this chant?
- Do you know that one?
- We've sung this before, remember?

- This is a new song.
- I have a chant for you today.
- We haven't sung it before.
- It may be new for most of you.

- This is a great song.
- This is one of my favorite chants.
- I'm sure you'll like it.

- First listen to it, and then we'll sing.
- Don't sing this time. Just listen. We'll sing in a minute.
- I'll play/sing it for you first. Just listen this time.
- Let's just listen this time, and then we'll sing it all together.

- Listen to the words.
- See how many of the words you can understand.
- Try to figure out the words.

- Fill in the blanks.
- Listen and write the missing words.

III. Language Practice

- As you listen, follow along and fill in the blanks.

- How many times do you hear 'sunshine'?
- This time, as you listen, I want you to count how many times the singer says 'sunshine'.
- Raise your hand every time you hear the word 'sunshine'.

- Let's go through the words.
- Let's look at the lyrics before we sing it.
- Don't worry about the tune, just say the words.

- Do you know all the words?
- Can you remember all the words?
- Do you know it by heart?
- Do you still need the words?
- Can you sing it without looking at the words?

- All right. Let's try it now.
- Let's do it together.
- Let's sing. Are you ready?
- I think we're ready to try singing it.
- I think we can do it. Shall we give it a try?

> **도움말**
>
> 노래나 챈트를 할 때는 학생들이 동시에 시작할 수 있도록 교사가 신호를 주면 도움이 됩니다.

- Ready... and...(학생들이 'and ...'에 이어서 시작할 수 있도록교사가 손으로 신호를 해주어야 한다.)
- 1... 2... ready... and...(학생들이 'and ...'에 이어서 시작할 수 있도록 교사가 손으로 신호를 해주어야 한다.)
- Ready... go...(교사가 'go'라고 말할 때 학생들이 시작할 수 있도록 손으로 신호를 해주어야 한다.)

- Uh... maybe we need a little more practice.
- Well, I think we can sing it a little better.
- Let's do it again. This time with more confidence.

- Sing along with the recording.
- I'll play the recording, and you sing along.
- Everyone sing along with the recording this time.

- Can we have a volunteer to sing the song?
- Who wants to sing it for us?
- Would anyone like to be a soloist today?

- Do the motions (along with the song).
- This time. let's do it with the motions.
- Try to do the movement as you sing.

III. Language Practice | 245

- Let's practice line by line.
- Let's practice the song one line at the time.
- Repeat each line after the recording.

- Clap along to the rhythm.
- Tap the rhythm on your desks.
- Let's clap on the strong beat.

> **도움말**
>
> 노래나 챈트 활동에 사용되는 단어들에는 verse, song words, chorus, rhythm 등이 있습니다.

19 Drawing
그림 그리기

> Teacher: We're going to do some drawing. Get out your colored pencils. Think about your dream house. What does it look like? Does it have a big yard? Is there a swimming pool? Draw a picture of your dream house.

- Now we get to draw pictures.
- We're going to do some drawing.
- Get ready to draw some pictures.

- Think about your dream house. What does it look like?
- I want you to imagine your dream house. What does it have in it?
- If you could design your own house, how would it look?

- Draw a picture of your dream house.
- I'd like you to draw your family.
- Imagine the kind of house you'd like to live in and draw a picture of it.

- Draw it quickly.
- Don't use a lot of detail.
- Just make a quick sketch.
- It doesn't have to be perfect.

- Color the picture.
- Color the circle yellow.
- Make the circle yellow.
- The circle should be yellow.

> **도움말**
>
> 색을 나타내는 단어는 형용사로만 사용되는 것이 아니라 명사로도 사용됩니다.
> 　　incorrect: *Make the circle yellow color.
> 　　correct:　 Make the circle yellow.

- Fold the paper in half.
- Fold the paper like this.
- Fold the paper down the middle.
- Fold the paper into four sections.

- Draw one picture in each section.

- Unfold it.
- Open it up.

- Cut out a triangle/the picture.
- Cut along the dotted line.
- Tear it along the perforated edge.

- Can I see?
- May I see what you've done?
- Can you show me your drawing?

- What's this?
- Guess what I'm drawing.
- Can you tell what this is?

PART IV

Using Teaching Aids and Electrical Equipment
교구 및 기자재 사용

PART IV

Using Teaching Aids and Electrical Equipment
교구 및 기자재 사용

1. Textbook 교과서 사용하기
2. Locating Pages 페이지 찾기
3. Locating Things on The Page 페이지에서 원하는 것 찾기
4. Blackboard/White Board/Magnet Board
   칠판/백판/자석판 사용하기
5. Word Cards 단어카드 사용하기
6. Picture Cards/Pictures 그림카드/사진 사용하기
7. Work Cards/Worksheets 워크카드/워크시트 사용하기
8. Information Gaps 정보차 활동하기
9. Flannel Board 융판 사용하기
10. Wall Pictures/Wall Posters 벽 그림/벽 포스터 사용하기
11. Newspapers/Publicity Materials 신문/광고자료 사용하기
12. Graphs, Charts, Maps 그래프, 도표, 지도 사용하기
13. Finger Puppets 손가락 인형 사용하기
14. Audio/Video Recordings 오디오 녹음/비디오 녹화자료 사용하기
15. Videotaping 녹화하기
16. Beam Projector/PPT 빔 프로젝터/PPT 기기 사용하기
17. Language Lab 어학실습실 사용하기
18. Computers 컴퓨터 사용하기
19. Problematic Equipment 기자재 문제/고장에 대하여 이야기하기

1 Textbook
교과서 사용하기

Teacher: Open your books to chapter 5. What page does chapter 5 start on?
Student: 35.
Teacher: Then everyone, turn to page 35. Are you all on page 35?
Student: Yes.
Teacher: Good. I'd like you to read the passage on this page. Before you start reading though, you should look at the questions at the end of the article. If you turn the page, you'll see the questions at the bottom of page 37.

- Take out your books, please.
- Please, get out your textbooks.
- Could you take your textbooks out?

- Who doesn't have a book?
◦ I don't.

- Sun-hee, share your book with Min-ho, please.
- Close your books.
- Put your books away.
- You may put your books away now.

2. Locating Pages
페이지 찾기

> Teacher: Let's look at page 35. Have you all found page 35?
> Students: Yes.
> Teacher: Good.

- Open your books to page 35.
- Let's look at page 35.
- Please take out your books and turn to page 35.

- Turn to page 35.
- Let's move on to page 35.
- Could you turn to page 35?

- Are you all on page 35?
- Have you all found the page?
- Are we all on the same page?
- Do you know where we are?
- Does everyone have the page?

- Next page, please.
- Let's go on to the next page.
- Look over at the next/right-hand page.
  (학생이 다음 페이지를 미리 볼 수 있을 때 'look (over) at'을 사용함)
- Turn the page.
  (다음 페이지가 현재 페이지의 뒷면일 때 'turn'을 사용함)
- Turn over, please.

- Turn back to page 15.
- Look back at the page we were on before.
- Let's go back to the last page.

- Turn inside the front cover.
- Open your books and look at the inside of the front cover.
- Look at the information just inside the cover.

- Turn to chapter 5.
- Could you open your books to chapter 5?
- Let's go on to chapter 5.

- What page is chapter 5 on?
- What page does chapter 5 start on?
- Where does chapter 5 begin?

3 Locating Things on the Page
페이지에서 원하는 것 찾기

On page 15, there's a word study.
You can see an illustration on the next page.
If you turn the page, you'll see the questions at the bottom.

- In chapter 5, find the dialogue/reading section/exercises/song/cartoon.
- Could you turn to the dialogue in chapter 5?
- Who can find the dialogue in chapter 5? What page is it on?

- Please turn to the comprehension check-up on page 15.
- Go to page 15 and look at the comprehension check-up.
- Would you look at the comprehension check-up on page 15?

> **도움말**
>
> 다음은 페이지에서 원하는 것을 찾을 때 사용되는 단어들입니다.
> first page, listening, speaking, reading, writing, exercises, word/words & expressions, pronunciation/sounds, test, tape scripts, dialogue, song, chant, game, poem, activity 1, cartoon, practice/communication activity, pictures, drawings, maps, table, figure, box, references/sources, word list, appendix/appendices, answer section/answer page, front cover/back cover, inside of the front/back cover, copyright page?, cover page, title page, table of contents, author(s), publisher, publishing date, preface, introduction, sources/bibliography

- The word study is on the right side.
- There's an illustration of the word on the right.
- Look at the bottom of the page.

- How are the words in column A like the words in column C?
- What's the difference between the words in column A and column C?
- How are the pictures on pages 79 and 80 alike? How are they different?
- Can you find any similarities or differences between the words in column A and C?

- Where is the illustration?
- Can you find the picture?
- Do you see the picture?

- What does the picture mean?

- What does the illustration tell you?
- What can you find out from the illustration?

- Paragraph two line one.
- Look at the beginning of the second paragraph.
- It's in the first line of the second paragraph.

- A few lines down.
- Go down a few more lines.
- It's a little further down on the page.
- About two lines from the bottom.
- Can you find the second line from the bottom?
- Would you look at the second to the last line on the page?

- The definition is at the bottom of the page.
- Look at the footnote at the bottom of the page.
- There's a footnote that has the definition.

(전치사의 활용)
- at the bottom/top of the page
- on the left/right of the page
- in the middle of the page
- in the front/back of a book

- The index is in the back.
- You can find the index in the back.
- You should refer to the audio scripts in the back.
- There's a word list in the back of the book which might help you.

4 Blackboard/White Board/Magnet Board
칠판/백판/자석판 사용하기

Teacher: Could I have a volunteer to write some sentences on the board? Ham-byul, Could you come to the board?
Student: Okay. What do I write?
Teacher: Write your answer for exercise number 1. And Sun-duk, could you come and write your answer for number 2. Hambyul, you can use this section of the board, and Sun-duk, you can write on that section over there.

- Look at the board.
- Everyone, look at the board, please.
- Look at the sentences on the board.
- Take a look at what's on the board.
- Could I draw your attention to the board?

- I used red chalk/marker for the question words.
- I wrote the question words in red.
- The red words are question words.

- You need to write this down.
- Copy this down in your notebooks.
- Please write down everything that's on the board.

- Myung-su, come to the board please.
- Ham-byul, could you come to the board?
- Eun-ha, I'd like you to come over to the board.

- Just use these markers.
- Don't use permanent markers on the white board.
- Only use white board markers on the white board.

- Write this word on the board, please.
- Could I have a volunteer to write some sentences on the board?
- Jae-myung, please come here and write your answer on the board.

○ What do I write?

- Sae-hyun, write on the left. Woo-song, write on the right.
- Ok-sun, you can use the left side of the board. And Eun-mi, would you write on the right?
- Sung-duk use this section of the board. Soo-gyung, you can write on that part over there.

- Divide the board into three parts.
- Please write on your own part of the board.
- Write in your own section.

- Could you look at (what's written on) the board?
- Take a look at what's on the board.
- Could I draw your attention to the sentences on the board?

- Is it okay if I erase this?
- Have you all got this in your notes?
- Are you ready for me to erase this?

- Please could someone erase the board?
- Would someone erase the board?
- Min-ho, will you erase the board?
- Would someone mind erasing the board?

- Erase that corner.
- Could you erase the words on the left at the top?
- Would you erase the top left-hand corner?

- Erase everything please.
- Clean off the whole board
- You don't need to leave anything up.

- Set this on the chalk/marker rail.
- Put the eraser back on the chalk rail.
- Would you line these pictures up on the chalk rail?

- Put this picture on the board, please.
- Could you stick this to the board?
- I'd like you to hang this picture on the board.

- Where should we put this?
- Where should this one go?
- Where do you want to put this one?

- And this one. Where should it go?
- Where should we put the next one?
- Where do you want this one to go?

- Please take the picture off the board.
- Could you take the picture down?
- Would you mind taking the picture off the board?

- Draw one on the board.
- Could you draw a picture of it on the board?
- Would you draw it for us on the board?

- What's this?
- Do you know what this is (a picture of)?
- Can you tell what the picture is on the board?

- Underline the word, please.
- Underline the subject.
- Draw a line under the word 'house'.

- Thank you. Go back to your seat, please.
- You may sit down now.
- Thanks. You can go back to your seat.

- Everyone, read this word.
- Let's read this all together.
- Let's read the words on the board.

- Again.
- Say it again.
- One more time.

- Copy these words into your notebooks.
- Write this down in your notebooks.
- You need to take notes on this.

5 Word Cards
단어카드 사용하기

Teacher: We're going to play a game with cards. Wait a second. I'll set up the cards. I need some help. Dong-myung and Jae-won, would you help me put up these cards?
Student: Okay. (교사가 카드 한 개를 집는다.) Where do I put it?
Teacher: (교사가 카드 붙일 곳을 가리킨다.) Stick the card up there. And Jae-won, would you stick this card on the wall? Good. Now point to the right card when you hear the word.

- Jae-ku, come up here and take a card please.
- Dong-myung, would you take a card from this set?
- Geum-jun, you need to get a card from the front of the room.

- I'll set up the cards.
- I'll put the cards upon the board.
- First let me put the cards on the chart.

- Stick the card up there.
- Put the card in the right place on the chart.
- Would you stick this card on the wall?
- Would you put the card up on the wall over there?
- The card should go up over there.
- Where does this card go? Would you stick it in the right place?

- Where do I put it?
- Where am I supposed to put it?

• Spread the cards out on your desk.
• Make sure you can see all of the cards.
• Turn all of the cards face down/up on your desk.

> **도움말**
>
> 카드의 앞면을 'face'라고 부릅니다. 카드 게임은 다음과 같습니다.
> 'If the cards are face up, the students can see the information on the cards. If the cards are face down, the information is hidden.'
> 추측게임의 경우는 다음과 같습니다.
> 'The students might place the cards face down if they are playing a guessing game.'

• What's on the back of the card?
• What information can you find on the back of the card?
• What does the back side of the card tell you?

> **도움말**
>
> 카드와 관련된 표현인 'on the front of the card'와 'on the back of the card' 구문을 이용하여 학생들에게 전치사를 효과적으로 설명해 줄 수 있습니다.

• Choose a card.
• Pick a card.
• Take a card. Any card.

- Mix up the cards.
- We need to mix up the cards.
- Could you shuffle?

- Who took this card?
- Who has this card?
- Who has the matching card?
- Did anyone get this card?

- What does this card say in Korean?
- What do the directions mean?
- Can you translate what this card says into Korean?

- Make a sentence using the word on the card.
- Fill in the blank with the word on the card.
- Use the word on the card as a cue.
- Use the word on the card to make a question.

- Point to the card when you hear the word.
- Find the card that matches the word you hear.
- When you hear the word, say the number of the card.
- When you hear the word, raise your card.

- The answer/word/sentence is on the back.
- You can find the correct answer on the back of the card.
- The back of the card has the answer.

- If you guess right, you can keep the card.
- If you get the right answer you can take the card.
- If you find the matching cards, your team can keep them.

4 Picture Cards/Pictures
그림카드/사진 사용하기

> Teacher: Look at the picture on page 78. How could you describe the picture? What words come to mind when you see the picture?
> Student: Dark.
> Teacher: Mm-hmm.
> Student: Scary.
> Student: Rainy.
> Teacher: Yes. Scary and rainy. What do you see in the picture?
> Student: People.
> Teacher: Right. People. Who are they? What are they doing?

- Look at this picture.
- Look at the picture in your book.
- Can you look at the people on page 78?
- Take a look at the people in the picture.

도움말

'Can you see the picture?' 라는 질문이 의미하는 것은 그림을 볼 수 있는 능력에 대해 묻는 것이므로, 학생들에게 검토해 보라는 의미로 물을 때에는 'Can you look at the picture?'라는 표현이 더 적절합니다.

- Describe the picture.
- How could you describe the picture?
- What feelings do you get when you see this picture?
- What words come to mind when you see look at this picture?

- What do you see?
- What do you see in this picture?
- Tell me what's in the picture.

- Who are they?
- What do they look like?
- What can you tell me about the people in the picture?

- Where are they?
- What kind of place is this?
- Where are the people in this picture?

- What are they doing?
- What's going on in this picture?
- What do you think is happening in this picture?
- What are they saying?
- What are they talking about?
- What do you think they're talking about?
- Can you guess what they're discussing?

- Look at the man with the red coat.
- Did you find the man with the red coat?
- Can you all see the man with the red coat?
- There's a man with a red coat at the bottom. Can you find him?

- Look at these two pictures. What's different?
- How are these two pictures different?
- Can you find the differences?
- What are the differences between these to pictures?

- There's a rabbit in this picture, but not in that one.
- This picture has a rabbit, but that one doesn't.
- Which picture has a rabbit?

- Put these in order.
- Arrange the parts of the story in order.
- What part comes first? What comes second?

- What's this (in Korean/English)?
- What do you call this (in English/Korean)?
- What is this a picture of?

7 Work Cards/Worksheets
워크카드/워크시트 사용하기

> Teacher: You and your partner should each have a different card. Read the instructions on your card. Your card tells you who you are. Then ask questions to your partner. Don't look at your partner's card. Listen to your partner.

- Read the directions on your worksheet/workcard.
- Look at the instructions on your card.
- Follow the directions on your card.

도움말

'instructions'와 'directions'는 복수형으로 사용하는 것을 주의할 필요가 있습니다.

- The worksheet/workcard tells you what you have to do.
- The card says how you should act.
- Look at your card. It says who you are.

- You should each have a different worksheet/workcard.
- You and your partner should have different cards.
- If your card is the same as your partner's, you need to change cards.

- Don't look at your partner's worksheet/workcard. Listen to your partner.
- Don't show each other your cards. Talk about them.
- Look at your own card. Ask your partner questions to get the information you need.

[Crossword puzzles and word searches]
- Solve the puzzle.
- Read the hint. Guess the word.
- Read the clue and try to figure out what word it is.

- Put one letter in each blank.
- You need to have one letter in each box.
- Write the first letter in this box, and the next letter in the next box, and so on.

- The words can go down, across, or diagonally.
- The word might go in three different directions.
- Some words might be backwards.

[Questionnaires]
- Copy this chart.
- Make a grid like this. Write the names at the top and write the questions along the side.
- Make a chart and fill in the questions along the side.

- Answer the questions on the questionnaire.
- Answer the questions about yourself.
- Write your own answers in the first column.

- Interview your partner.
- Ask the questions to your partner.
- Find a partner and ask them the questions.

- Record your partner's answer.
- Check whether your partner says 'yes' or 'no'.
- Write down what your partner says.

- You should interview at least three people.
- Make sure you talk to at least three different people.
- Go around the room and get answers from at least three different people.

8 Information Gaps
정보차 활동하기

> Teacher: You and your partner have different information. Work together. Ask your partner questions and then fill in the missing information in your own chart.

- You and your partner have different clues about the story.
- You have some of the information and your partner has some of the information.
- Some of you have Beth's schedule and some of you have Bill's schedule.

- Tell your teammates about the paragraph you read.
- Summarize your card for your group.
- Tell the rest of your group about the information you have on your card.

- Work together.
- You have to help each other.
- You have to ask each other questions to figure out the answer.
- You need to share your answers to solve the puzzle.

- Ask your partner questions and then fill in the missing information on your own chart.
- Use your partner's information to figure out the answer.
- After your partner tells you about the other option, you can decide which option is better.

9 Flannel Board
융판 사용하기

Teacher: I'm going to tell you a story. Let me get out the flannel board. Okay, let's begin. Once upon a time...

- Let me get out the flannel board.
- Can you help me set up the flannel board?
- Let's put the flannel board over here.

- I need the felt pieces.
- Would you hand me the felt?
- I need to use these pictures.

10 Wall Pictures/Wall Posters
벽 그림/벽 포스터 사용하기

Teacher: Would you hang this poster over there? Here is some tape. Thanks, that's good. Now class, look at the poster.

- Hang the poster/picture up over there, please.
- Could I have a volunteer to hang the poster up?
- Would you hang this poster over there for me?

- Do you need tape?
- You'll need to get some tape.
- Maybe you should use a staple gun.

- Look at the poster/picture.
- I have a picture for you today.
- Could you look at the poster on the wall?

11 Newspapers/Publicity Materials
신문/광고자료 사용하기

Teacher: Let's move on to some reading. I took this out of the newspaper for you to read. First look at the headline. Mun-yeong, would you read the headline for us.
Student: 'New Discovery Brings Hope.'
Teacher: Thanks. Can you guess what the article is about?

도움말

신문이나 광고자료를 이용할 때 사용되는 단어에는 headline, by-line, comic strip, frame, editorial, advertisement 등이 있습니다.

- How often do you read the newspaper?
- Do you read the newspaper at home?
- Do you ever look at English newspapers?

- Which paper?
- Which newspaper do you usually read?
- What paper does your family subscribe to?

- I brought a newspaper article for you today.
- We're going to look at some newspaper articles today.
- I took this out of the newspaper for you to read.
- When was this article written?
- Can you find the date?
- What's the date on this article?

- Which section is this?
- Is this the sports section? What about the editorial section?
- What section does this belong to?

- What section do you like? Why?
- What section do you usually read first? Why do you like it?
- Do you usually start at the back or the front when you read the newspaper?

- Turn to the weather/culture section.
- Find the section that says 'culture' at the top.
- Can you find the weather/culture section of the newspaper?

- Where are the TV programs/movies listed?
- Can you find the TV/movie listings?
- Where would you find out when a certain movie was playing/a certain TV show was on?

- What articles/advertisements do you see on the first page?
- Look for the advertisements on the first page.
- What are the articles about on the first page?

- First look at the headline.
- What does the headline say?
- Look at the title at the top of the page.

- Can you guess what the article is about?
- Why do you think these people are famous?
- What do you think the story talks about?

- Read the article.
- Scan through the article.
- Try to read the article in 10 minutes.
- Go ahead and read the article as fast as you can.

- Put the paragraphs/sentences in order.
- Rearrange these paragraphs/sentences.
- These paragraphs/sentences are mixed up. Try to figure out what order they come in.

- Choose the best title for the article.
- Read the titles. Decide which one fits the article best.
- Try to think of a title for the article.
- I'd like you to make up a title for the article.
- Write the best title under the picture.
- Write the caption under the picture.
- Match the captions with the right pictures.

- What are the characters saying in this cartoon?
- Look at the cartoon. Imagine what the characters are saying.
- Write your own dialogue in the speech bubbles.

- Write a reply to the ad.
- You have to write a response to this ad.
- Imagine how you would respond to an advertisement like this.

12 Graphs, Charts, Maps
그래프, 도표, 지도 사용하기

Teacher: What does this graph show?
Student: People. Years.
Teacher: Yes, it shows the number of people who attended the camp in different years. Look at the first column. What year is it?
Student: 2011.
Teacher: Yes, and look at the second column over. What year is that?
Student: 2012.
Teacher: Were there more people or fewer people at the camp in 2012 than in 2011?
Student: More people.

- What is this graph/chart/map about?
- What does the chart show?
- What information can you find on this map?
- What two things does this graph compare?

- What information is in the first column?
- What does the first column tell you about?
- What can you find out in the first column?

- Look at the second column, second row.
- Find the second row down, one column over.
- Now let's look at the second column.

- What happened between 2011 and 2012?
- How does the graph change between 2011 and 2012?
- What's different in the last column?

- Why does the line go up really fast here?
- How come the line doesn't go up very much after 2012?
- What do you think the sharp increase/decline since 2012 tells us?
- What can we learn from this part of the graph?

> **도움말**
>
> 다음은 그래프, 도표, 지도를 활용할 때 사용되는 표현들입니다.
> graph - line graphs, bar graphs, and pie graphs show proportional relationships
> chart - has information in rows and columns
> map   - shows land, usually from an areal view

- The legend tells you what the pictures mean.
- The key shows what the symbols mean on the map.
- The key gives the meaning for all the pictures.

13 Finger Puppets
손가락 인형 사용하기

Teacher: This is Mrs. Bear and this Goldilocks. Can you all say, 'Hello' to Mrs. Bear?
Students: Hello.
Teacher: Very good. Now it's your turn to make finger puppets. Draw a face on your finger like this. (학생들이 손가락에 그림을 그린다.) Wonderful. (교사가 한 학생의 손가락을 바라본다.) What's his name?
Student: Boo boo.
Teacher: Oh. Hi, Boo boo. Can your finger say, 'Hi, I'm Boo boo?'
Student: Hi. I'm Boo boo.

- This is Mrs. Bear and this is Goldilocks. (introducing the puppets.)
- Here is Mrs. Bear.
- Who do you think this is? It's Mrs Bear!

- Say, 'hello' to Mrs. Bear.
- Can you all say, 'Hello' to Mrs. Bear?
- Now why don't you all say, 'Hello' to each other?

도움말

'say'라는 동사는 항상 직접목적어와 함께 사용해야합니다. 그러므로 'Say to Mrs. Bear.'과 같은 표현은 틀린 표현입니다.

- Let's make our own finger puppets!
- Now it's your turn to make finger puppets.
- I want you all to make finger puppets like mine.

- Please draw faces on your fingers.
- Draw a face on your finger— like this.
- Draw a different face on each finger.

- Take the puppets off.
- You have to take the puppets off now.
- We're finished playing with the puppets now.

- What's his name?
- What's this puppet's name?
- Let me see your second finger. Okay! What's this guy's name?

- What's the tiger's name?
- What did you name your tiger puppet?
- Does the tiger have a name? What is it?

- Make your fingers say, 'hi'.
- Can your finger say, 'Hi, I'm Sue'?
- Make your puppet introduce herself.
- Make your fingers bow and say, 'hello' to each other.

- Wiggle your fingers.
- Let's warm up our fingers.
- Practice moving your fingers now.

- Practice talking with your puppets.
- Now have your puppets say the whole thing.
- Can your puppets do the whole conversation?

> **도움말**
>
> 다음은 손가락 인형을 활용할 때 사용되는 표현들입니다.
> thumb, index finger/pointer finger, long finger/middle finger, ring finger, little finger/pinky knuckle, back of your hand, palm, finger nails, finger tips, wrist

14 Audio/Video Recordings
오디오 녹음/비디오 녹화 자료 사용하기

Teacher: We're going to watch a video. Could somebody turn the lights off. (한 학생이 불을 끈다.) Thanks. We'll watch it without the sound this time. I just want you to watch what the characters do. We'll listen later. Let's watch the clip. (교사가 비디오를 작동시킨다.) What did you see?
Student: A police officer and a little girl.
Teacher: Right. What do you think they were saying?

- Watch the video.
- Let's listen to the recording now.
- Are you ready to watch the video?

- Pay attention to this part.
- Pay close attention here.
- This is part is important, so listen closely.
- Listen carefully and try to figure out exactly what they're saying.

- I want you to listen for the answer.
- Try to answer this as you're watching.
- Think about these questions as you watch and try to figure out the answers.
- Let's watch it once.
- I'll play it for you one time.

IV. Using Teaching Aids and Electrical Equipment | 285

- I'm only going to play this once/twice, so listen carefully.

- I'll play the recording now.
- Here is the video.
- Listen to the recording.
- I'd like you to listen to the recording.
- Let's watch the clip.
- Are you ready to see the video?

- We'll watch it without the sound/picture this time.
- I just want you to watch what the characters do. We'll listen later.
- I'm going to play the clip with the sound off. Just look at the picture.

- Here it is.
- Here it comes.
- It's starting now.

- Shh. Listen.
- Be quiet. It's time to listen.
- Stop talking so you can hear this.

- Did you hear/see the ...?

- Listen/Watch again.
- I'll play it again.
- Let's listen one more time.

- Listen/Watch and answer the questions.
- Write the answers as you're watching.
- Try to listen for the answers to these questions.

- Listen and repeat.
- Repeat each line after the recording.
- When the man on the recording says, 'How are you?' then you say, 'How are you?'

- What did you see/hear?
- Tell me about what you saw/heard?
- Can you describe what happened?

- What were the characters talking about?
- What do you think they were saying?
- Can you guess what they were arguing about?

- What do you think you will see on the video?
- Where do you think the action took place?
- Can you guess what you will see when I show you the picture?

- Half of you are going to see the picture and half of you are going to hear the sound only.
- I want half of you to watch the screen and half of you to just listen to the sound.
- You on this side of the room will get to see the picture, and you on that side of the room should just listen.

- Find a partner and tell them about what you saw/heard.
- Please talk to someone else about what you saw.
- If you were just listening, find a partner and tell them what you think what you would see.

- Let's watch it again.
- Would you like to see it again?
- Shall we watch it again?

- Is the volume okay?
- Is it too soft?
- Is it loud enough?
- Ji-nah, can you hear?
- Is there anyone who can't here?

- I'll have to turn the volume up.
- Then I'll turn it up a bit. How's that?
- Okay then. I'll turn the volume a little higher.

- We should turn on/off the lights.
- We need the lights off.
- Let's turn the lights on.
- Could somebody get the lights? (on or off)
- Okay, we can have the lights back on now.
- Would somebody turn the lights back on?
- Woo-sung, would you turn the lights off for me?

- Can you see in the back?
- Can everyone see the screen?
- Raise your hand if you can't see.
- Can you see the screen from where you're sitting?

- Oh. There's a glare across the screen.
- There's a glare from the windows.
- We need to close the shades to get rid of the glare.

- Oops. Wrong place/track.
- Oops. We're in the wrong place.
- Oh. That's not where I wanted to start.
- We need a different track.

- Wait. I'm finding the place/track.
- Wait a second while I find the right scene.
- Just give me a moment. I'm looking for the right place.

- Let me pause the recording.
- We'll stop here for a minute.
- Are there any questions while I pause the movie?

- When you see your character, say the right expression.
- When your character is on the screen, say his or her lines.
- When your character is talking, say what he or she is saying.

15 Videotaping
녹화하기

> Teacher: We're going to record this class. Eun-ji, I'd like you to be our camera person today. Would you record this for us?
> Student: Okay.
> Teacher: Let's put the camera over there.

- The class is going to be recorded today.
- Someone will come in and record our class.
- We're going to record this class.

- Let's put the camera over here.
- Could you move the video camera over there?
- I'd like you stand in the back of the room while you're recording.

- I'd like you to zoom in on this area.
- Could you focus in on this area?
- Why don't you focus on the teacher/students?

- Would you record this?
- I'd like you to be the camera person today.
- Can you hold the video camera and record this for us?

16 Beam Projector/PPT
빔 프로젝터/PPT 기기 사용하기

Teacher:	First we need to set up the beam projector. Would you plug it in?
Student:	Sure. (학생이 빔 프로젝터를 전원에 연결한다.)
Teacher:	Thanks. Could someone pull the screen down?
Student:	Okay. (학생이 스크린을 내린다.)
Teacher:	Great. Now we need to adjust the focus. (교사가 초점을 맞추고 그림이 선명해진다.) There. That's good.

- First we need to set up the beam projector.
- We can put it on this desk.
- Would you plug it in?

- We need to have the screen down.
- Could someone pull down the screen?
- We can project against the wall.

- Let me focus it.
- Could you focus it?
- We need to adjust the focus.
- Is it clear yet?

(조정이 잘 되었을 때)
- There.
- That's good.
- Great.

- Press 'Enter'.
- Let's go to the next slide.
- Please advance to the next slide.

- Let me show you the answers.
- The answers are on the screen.
- You can see the answers on the screen.

17 Language Lab
어학실습실 사용하기

Teacher: Welcome to the language lab. Each station should have a headset and a microphone. Does everyone have a microphone?
Student: Yes.
Teacher: Good. Then turn you microphone on and put on your headset. Can you all hear?

- Each station should have a headset and a microphone.
- There should be a headset and a microphone for everyone.
- Does everyone have a headset and a microphone?
- Raise your hand if you need a headset.

○ I don't have a headset.
○ I need a microphone.

- Turn your microphone on.
- Is your microphone turned on?
- Please make sure your microphone is on.

- Put on your headsets.
- Let's do this with your headsets on.
- You'll need your headsets.
- You should wear your headsets for this activity.

- Can you all hear?
- Does your headset work?
- Can you hear with your earphones?
- Are you having problems with your headphones?

> **도움말**
> 'earphones'와 'headphones'는 항상 복수형으로 사용됩니다.

○ I can't hear.
○ My headset doesn't work.

- Press the red button to talk.
- Press the red button if you want to speak.
- You need to press the red button to speak.

- I'm going to put you in groups.
- You will be able to hear the other people at your table.
- You will be connected with the other people at your table.

18 Computers
컴퓨터 사용하기

Teacher: Today we are going to use the computer to learn about earthquakes. You're going to run a search for some information on the Internet. I'd like you to find a Website that tells about earthquakes. First open the Internet browser. Double click on the icon. Good. Now type your key-word in the box. What are we going to study today?
Student: Earthquakes.
Teacher: Yes, earthquakes. So type 'earthquakes' in the box and press enter.

- Turn on the computer and the monitor.
- Press the power button.
- Make sure both your computer and your monitor are on.

- Wait for the computer to get started.
- Wait a second while the computer boots up.
- Just wait while the computer gets started.

- Put the USB stick in.
- Put the USB stick in the USB drive.
- Find the USB drive and put the USB stick in.

- Open 'Fun with English'.
- Double click on the 'Fun With English' icon.
- First you have to get out the 'Fun with English' application.

- Select 'new game' under 'options'.
- Go to the 'options' menu at the top of the screen and select 'new game'.
- Do you see 'options'? Okay. Now go down the menu and select 'new game'.
- Click on 'options'. Now hold the mouse button down until you get to 'new game'.

- Open the Internet browser.
- We're going to do some work on the Internet today.
- I thought we could use the Internet today.

- We are going to use the computer to learn about bears.
- I'd like you to find some information on-line about bears.
- We're going to use the Internet to find some information about bears.

- You're going to run a search for some information on the Internet.
- To do this assignment, you'll need to search for several things on the Internet.

- Find a website about ... .
- I'd like you to find a website that shows ... .
- Try to find a page that shows tells about ... .

- Type your key-word in the box.
- Type 'earthquakes' in the box and then press enter.
- Type in your key-word and then click on 'search'.
- What do you want to find information about? Okay, type that in the box.

- You need to click on the hypertext to follow the link.
- If you click on the hypertext, you'll go directly to the page.
- Click on the blue letters and that should take you to the page you want.

- I want you to go to this website.
- Here is the address that I'd like you to look up.
- This the address for the web page that I want you to visit.

- Print the information you found.
- Go to 'file' and select 'print' from the menu.

- Visit the chat room.
- I'd like you to try the chat room.
- If you go to this site, you can chat with other students in English.

- You need to download this program.
- First scan for viruses and then download.
- You can click on download.

- You need to open your e-mail account.
- You have to get into your e-mail account.
- Enter your login name and your password.

- Your subject should be 'subscribe'.
- I want you to use 'subscribe' as the subject.
- Please type 'subscribe' in the subject line.

- Send me a copy of the message.
- Type my address in the CC box.
- I'd like you to send a copy of your message to my account.

- Send it.
- Okay. You can send the message now.
- When you're all finished, click 'send'.

- You can logout now.
- All right. It's time to logout.
- I'd like you to close the program and logout.

- Remember to shut down.
- Don't forget to shut the computer down before you turn it off.
- When you're ready to finish, select 'shut down' from the 'start' menu.

> **도움말**
>
> 다음은 컴퓨터를 활용할 때 사용되는 단어입니다.
> mouse, screen, monitor, keyboard, Internet, web page, website, home page, e-mail

19 Problematic Equipment
기자재 문제/고장에 대하여 이야기하기

> Teacher: Are you ready to listen? (교사가 'audio file'을 열고 'play' 버튼을 누른다.) Okay, here it is. (소리가 나지 않는다.) That's funny. It doesn't seem to be working.

- That's funny. It doesn't seem to be working.
- What's wrong? Why isn't it playing?
- This is weird. It isn't working right.

- Where's the power switch?
- How do I turn it on?
- Where does it turn on?

- The computer screen is frozen.
- The pointer isn't responding to the mouse.

- It won't play/run.
- It's stuck.

- It isn't plugged in.
- It isn't connected.

- Just be patient while I fix this.
- Hang on a second while I try to figure this out.
- It'll be okay. I'm working on it.

IV. Using Teaching Aids and Electrical Equipment | 299

- Does anybody know anything about computers?
- Does anyone know how to run this?
- Can anyone give me a hand?

- Could you go and ask someone to fix the computer?
- Could you find someone to take care of the computer?
- Would you go and ask Mr. Shin to look at the computer?

- We'll have to use a different machine.
- We need to get another beam projector.
- I think you should move to a different computer.
- Maybe you can use that headset.

- Maybe we'll have to skip the video today.
- We'll just have to do something else.
- Oh, that's too bad. Why don't we move on to ...?

PART V

Consolidation of the Lesson
수업 강화

PART V

Consolidation of the Lesson
수업 강화

1. Review of the Lesson 복습하기
2. Testing: Exams and Quizzes 평가: 시험 및 퀴즈보기
3. NEAT Speaking Activities 국가영어능력평가시험의 말하기 활동하기
4. Giving Homework 숙제 부과하기

1. Review of the Lesson
복습하기

Teacher:	Okay. So what did we talk about today?
Student:	Wishing.
Teacher:	Right. Today we learned how to talk about things we wish for. Do you have any questions about what we learned today?
Student:	I have a question.
Teacher:	Okay.
Student:	What's the difference between 'wish' and 'hope'?
Teacher:	Well, you use 'wish' for things that aren't true and you use 'hope' for things that might be true. I wish I were taller but I hope you all do well on your test tomorrow. Do you get it?
Student:	I think so.
Teacher:	I had a good time today. I hope you had as much fun as I did.

- Let's review what we did today.
- What did we do with ... ?
- Okay. So what did we talk about today?
- It's time to review today's lesson.

- I think we should go over this one last time.
- Do you remember what we did way back at the beginning of the class?

V. Consolidation of the Lesson

- We learned ... today.
- Today we learned how to ...
- Now you know how to ...

- Do you get it? (Got it./Not really.)
- Do you think you can ... ?
- Do you feel like you understand what we did today?

  ○ I think so./Not really.

- We'll come back to it tomorrow.
- You'll get some more practice later on.
- We'll go over this again before the test.

- Any questions?
- Do you have any questions about what we learned today?
- Are there any questions about the material we've covered so far?

  ○ I have a question.
  ○ Can I ask a question?
  ○ I have a question about page 55.

- You worked hard today.
- You did a good job today. I'm very happy with what we did.
- Thanks for concentrating so well today. I'm thoroughly impressed.

- You're getting better every day!
- Your English is getting better and better.
- You have improved so much since the beginning of the semester.
- You've made so much progress.
- Every time I see you, you can speak better than the day before.

- This has been fun.
- This was a good class.
- I had a good time today. I hope you had as much fun as I did.

> **도움말**
>
> 북미권 선생님들은 학생들에게 수업에 관하여 'Did you have fun?' 이라고 질문하지 않습니다. 이 질문은 학생들이 부정적(No, it was boring.)으로 답할 수 있는 여지를 줄 수 있고, 얼마나 많이 배웠는지 보다는 재미의 측면에서만 수업을 평가할 수 있기 때문입니다.

2 Testing: Exams and Quizzes
평가: 시험 및 퀴즈보기

Student: When is the test?
Teacher: The test is on Thursday. The test will cover chapters 2 and 3. Please review the material at home with your CD-ROM.
Students: Yes.

- We are going to have a test on this.
- You should start thinking about the test.
- We have an exam coming up.

- It's not a big test.
- It's just a little quiz.
- It won't be very long— just ten questions.

(시험에 관한 발표가 있기 전)
◦ When is the test?
◦ When are we going to have a test?

- It'll be next week Thursday.
- The test is on Thursday.
- You can expect a test on Thursday.

- Please review the lesson at home with the CD-ROM.
- Practice what we've learned today at home with the CD-ROM.
- Do the activities on the CD-ROM at home to review today's lesson.

> **도움말**
>
> 다음은 시험의 종류를 나타내는 단어입니다.
>
> exam, test, quiz, mid-term exam, final exam, practice test, achievement test, assessment test, aptitude test

- Do you want to know what's on the test?
- Do you want me to tell you about the test?
- Would you like me to tell you what's on the test?

○ What's on the test?
○ What's the test going to be on?
○ What's going to be on the test?

> **도움말**
>
> 교사는 학생들이 알고자 하는 것이 있는지를 아래와 같은 질의응답을 통하여 알아볼 수 있습니다. 학생은 질문을 통하여 언어를 배울 수 있습니다.
>
> For example:
>
>   Teacher: Do you want to know what's on the test?
>   Student: Yes.
>   Teacher: Then ask me: What's on the test?
>   Student: What's on the test?
>   Teacher: Capitalization will be on the test.

- Capitalization will be on the test.
- You should review the vocabulary from chapter 3 for the test.
- The test is going to cover chapters 2 and 3.

- Will this be on the test?

- This will be on the test.
- You can expect to see a question like this on the test.
- There might be a question like this on the test.
- It would be a good idea to study this. It might be on the test.
- You should probably review this ― just in case there's a surprise quiz.

◦ How are you going to test us?
◦ What kind of questions are going to be on the test?

- There will be some multiple choice.
- The test will have some multiple choice questions.
- The first part of the test will be multiple choice.

> **도움말**
> 다음은 시험 문항의 형태를 나타내는 표현입니다.
> objective question, multiple choice, fill in the blank, true/false, matching, dictation

- Are you ready for the test?
- Do you have any (last) questions before we begin?
- Is there anything I can help you with before we start?

- If you get stuck, just go on and come back to it later.
- If you don't know the answer just move on to the next problem.
- Don't spend all your time on one question.

- How much time do we have?

- You will have 40 minutes to finish the test.
- We'll stop at 9:40.
- I'll give you 40 minutes to finish this test.

- You may begin.
- You may start now.
- Go ahead and start working.

- There are 5 minutes remaining.
- There are only 5 minutes left.
- You have 5 minutes.
- If you're finished, check over your work.
- Look over the whole test in case you want to change something.

- It's time to finish up.
- Finish up what you're doing and then stop.
- Finish the question you're working on and then stop.

- All right. It's time to stop.
- You have to stop now.
- Put your pencils down and turn your papers over.

- I'm going to return your tests now.
- Here are your tests.
- Would you come up here and get your test when I call your name?

- Trade papers with a friend.
- Give your paper to someone else.
- Could you exchange papers with someone sitting near you?

- We'll correct the papers together.
- Let's go over the answers together.
- Shall we check the answers as a class?

- Check the answers in the back of the book.
- The answers are on the answer sheet.
- I'll put the right answers up on the screen.

- Please circle the right answers.
- I'd like you to mark your friend's paper.
- Please take out a different color pen, and check your friend's answers.

- What's the answer for number 1?
- What do you have for number 1?
- What did you get for the first question?
- Tell us what you wrote for first answer.
- How did you answer the first question?

- Is that right?
- Are there any other answers?
- Did anyone get anything else?
- Is there anything else that works?

- 'Fantastic' and 'fabulous' are both okay.
- Both of those answers are fine.
- Don't take any points away for that.

- 2 points for a perfect answer.
- These questions are 2 points each.
- You can get up to 2 points for each answer.

- Count up your/their points.
- Count how many points you got.
- Add up how many you got right.

- Who got more than 10 right?
- Did anyone have more than 10 right answers?
- Raise your hand if you got more than 10 right.

- There were 100 points on the test.
- The score was out of 100.
- You shouldn't have a score over 100.

- This test counts for 30% of your grade.
- This test will be 30% of your grade.
- 30% of your grade comes from this test.

- 80 points is a B.
- 80% is a B.
- If you got 80 out of 100, that's a B.
- The 80's are in the B range.

- Most of you did very well.
- The tests were pretty good.
- I was happy with the tests.
- It looks like you studied very hard.

- I think we'll need to review this material a bit more.
- The tests weren't very good this time.
- I don't think you knew the material very well.

3 NEAT Speaking Activities
국가영어능력평가시험의 말하기 활동하기

- Answer each question in one or two sentences.
- Give a short answer to each question.
- You only need to say one or two sentences for each question.

- Look at the pictures and tell a story.
- Tell a story about the pictures.
- Tell a story based on the pictures you see.

- Listen to the situation and then explain what you would do.
- Give advice based on the situation you hear.
- After you hear the story, you will need to give some advice.

- You have 60 seconds to prepare.
- You can think about your answer for 1 minute.
- You may take 1 minute to plan your answer.

- You will have 60 seconds to speak.
- You will have 1 minute to record your answer.
- Your answer will be recorded for 1 minute.

- Begin speaking when you hear a beep.
- When you hear a beep, it's time to start speaking.
- The beep is your signal to begin.

- Stop speaking when you hear two beeps.
- When you hear two beeps you may stop speaking.
- Two beeps mean that the time is up.

- Try to say as much as you can.
- Try to fill all of the time available.
- It's important to keep talking for the whole minute.

4 Giving Homework
숙제 부과하기

> Teacher: I have some homework for you. I'm giving you three options. You may do the assignment of your choice. This is group work, so divide up the work equally among members of your group. The whole group gets the same grade.
> Student: When is this due?
> Teacher: You can turn it in on Friday.

- There is homework.
- I have some homework for you.
- This is what you have to do for next class.
- I'd like you to do this at home.

- This ... is homework.('homework'는 불가산명사임)
- You need to do the exercises on page 6 at home.
- Please finish writing your questions for class tomorrow.

- This is individual/group work.
- You have to do this alone/with a partner/with your group.
- Work alone/together with your group.

- One grade per group.
- Everyone in your group/you and your partner will receive the same grade.
- The whole group gets the same grade.

- Divide up the work equally among the members of your group.
- Everyone in the group should do same amount of work.
- Make sure you split up the work evenly.
- Don't let one person do all the work. You have to work together.

- Choose one of the options to do as homework.
- You may do the assignment of your choice.
- Pick one of the options to do at home.

- Are there any questions about the homework?
- Are you all clear on the assignment?
- Does everyone understand what you have to do for tomorrow?

○ When is this due?

- This is due on Friday.
- You can turn it in on Friday.
- You need to get this to me by Friday.
- You have until Friday to finish this.

> **도움말**
> 'by'와 'until'은 맞바꾸어서 사용할 수 없습니다. 'until'은 'You have until Friday.' 나 'You may work on it until Friday.' 와 같이 정해진 기간까지 지속적으로 진행하는 경우에 사용하지만, 'by'는 'Turn it in by 8:00 on Friday.'나 'Get it to me by 8:00 on Friday.'처럼 정해진 기간 이전에 일어난 일을 표현할 때 사용합니다.

- Don't forget.
- Please remember to do this.
- Remember to bring it to class next time.

- This assignment is worth 10 points.
- I'll give you 10 points for doing the assignment
- You can earn up to 10 points with this assignment.

- You have to turn in your assignments twice during the semester.
- There are 2 important deadlines that you need to remember.
- There are 2 projects that you need to do this term.

- The first assignment is due on the fourth week, and the second on the tenth.
- You should turn in the first assignment 3 weeks from now.
- You need to submit your journal on October 10 and November 27.

- Let me explain the grading policy.
- This is the grading policy.
- This is how your assignments will be evaluated.

- Creativity is worth 5% of your grade.
- The degree of completeness counts as 5% of your grade.
- Do you use diverse references? Your references are 5% of your grade.
- Make sure you record and edit everything. Recording and editing are worth 5% of your grade.

- No homework today.
- I'm not going to give you any homework this time.
- Guess what? You don't have any homework today.

PART VI

The End of the Lesson
수업 종료

PART VI
The End of the Lesson
수업 종료

1. Almost Time to Stop 종료 시간이 다가옴을 알리기
2. Stop Working 활동 종료하기
3. Preparation for the Next Class 다음 수업 준비하기
4. Collecting Materials 교재 수거하기
5. Cleaning Up 정리하기
6. Ending the Lesson 수업 종료하기
7. Seasonal Greetings 절기 인사하기
8. Saying Goodbye 작별 인사하기

1. Almost Time to Stop
종료 시간이 다가옴을 알리기

Teacher: We're almost out of time. We just have a few more minutes, so I'd like to talk about the homework for tomorrow. I'd like you to finish the exercises on page 6, okay? Do you have any last questions before we go? Anyone?

- It's almost time to stop.
- It's just about time to go.
- We're almost out of time.
- We only have 5 more minutes.

도움말

'5 more minutes'가 '5 minutes more'보다 더 일반적인 표현입니다.

- There's only a little bit of time left, so I'd just like to mention a few things.
- We just have a few more minutes, so let's talk about the homework for tomorrow.
- Do you have any last questions before we go?

- We've finished a little early today.
- It looks like we have a little extra time today.
- I think we have time for one more thing.

- Let's end with a game.
- Let's play one last game.
- Before you go, let's play a quick game.
- Last but not least, we'll do a round of 'Simon Says'.

- Don't go yet.
- It isn't time to go yet.
- We still have to do one more thing.

- We'll work on this some more next time.
- We'll finish this next class.
- Let's stop here for now. We'll start here again next time.

2. Stop Working
활동 종료하기

Teacher: You may stop what you're working on. That's all we have time for today. Look at the time. We have to go.

- You can stop there.
- Stop what you're doing.
- You may stop what you're working on.

- Okay. It's time to stop.
- That's all we have time for today.
- It looks like we have to stop now.
- Look at the time. We have to go.
- It's time to stop already. That went fast.

3 Preparation for the Next Class
다음 수업 준비하기

> Teacher: Listen. I have a few things to tell you. We're going to take a field trip, remember? So you each need to bring 3,000 won to class tomorrow. This is important. If you don't take money, you can't go along, so don't forget. Now, how much money are you supposed to bring?
> Students: 3000 won.
> Teacher: And when are you going to bring it?
> Students: Tomorrow.
> Teacher: Good.

- I have a few things to tell you.
- I have a couple of announcements to make.
- There are some important things for you to know

- We're going to ...
- Get ready for a ... tomorrow.
- I have something special planned for tomorrow. We're going to ...

- Next time I'd like you to bring a ruler to class.
- You need to cut out an article form an English newspaper and bring it to class next time.
- Don't forget to have your parents sign this form.
- Please get your parents' signature at the bottom of this form.

- You each need to bring 3,000 won tomorrow.

> **도움말**
>
> 'sign'과 'signature'라는 표현을 사용할 때는 주의해야 할 필요가 있습니다. 'signature'는 사람의 이름을 손으로 쓰는 것을 의미합니다.
> incorrect: *Get your parent's sign.
> correct:　　Get your parent's signature.

- This is important.
- Don't forget.
- Remember to ...

4 Collecting Materials
교재 수거하기

> Teacher: I'd like the cards back. So-ra, would you collect the cards for me?
> Student: Okay.
> Teacher: So-ra will come around and collect the cards. Give your cards to So-ra, She's collecting them.
> Student: (So-ra에게 카드를 건네며) Here you are.

- I'd like the cards back.
- Pass your papers to the front.
- Could I have your puppets before you leave?
- Remember to turn in your tapes.

- So-ra, would you collect the books for me? Okay.
- So-ra will come around and collect the scissors.
- Give your glue sticks to So-ra. She's (in charge of) collecting them.

◦ Here you are.

- Do I have all the cards?
- Does anyone still have a card?
- Is there anyone who hasn't handed in their card yet?

5. Cleaning Up
정리하기

Teacher: Let's clean up. Pack up your things. Check under your desks. Make sure there isn't anything on the floor. Throw all of the trash away. Oh, there's still something on the floor.
Student: Where?
Teacher: There, in the corner. Okay. Everything looks good.

- Pack up your things.
- You can put your things away now.
- Why don't you put your books and papers away?

- Don't forget anything.
- Don't leave anything behind.
- Don't leave any pens, pencil cases, notebooks...
- Make sure you take all your things with you.

도움말

'note'(노트)와 'notebook'(노트북)을 사용할 때는 주의를 요합니다. 'note'는 글로 기록한 정보이고, 'notebook'은 필기를 위한 책이므로 학생들은 'notebook'에 필기를 합니다. 그러므로 'Students write notes in a notebook.'라는 표현이 가능합니다.

- Let's clean up.
- We have a few minutes to straighten up.
- Please take a few minutes and put everything away.

- Check under your desks.
- Is there anything under your desks?
- Make sure there isn't anything left on the floor.

- Let's pick up the scrap paper.
- Throw all of the trash away.
- Would you pick up the scraps and put them in the wastebasket?

- Put the books over there.
- The books go on the shelf.
- Arrange the books neatly on the shelf.

- There's still something on the floor.
- I see something that hasn't been put away yet.
- There's still something that needs to be put away.
- Does that belong on the floor? Where does it go?

- Nice work. It looks good.
- Okay. Everything looks good.
- Good. The room looks clean.
- Okay. I think you're finished now.

6 Ending the Lesson
수업 종료하기

Teacher: Nice work today. We're done. You may go.

- We're done.
- All right. I think that's everything.
- That wraps it up.

- Nice work today.
- You worked hard today. Thanks.
- Thanks for concentrating today.

- It's time to go.
- You may go.
- You're dismissed.

7 Seasonal Greetings
절기 인사하기

> Teacher: Have a good Chuseok. Are you doing anything special? Are you going to visit relatives or stay home and play video games?
> Student: I'm going to visit relatives.
> Teacher: Where do you your relatives live?
> Student: In Busan.
> Teacher: Oh ... that's a long drive, isn't it?

- Happy birthday!

도움말

생일을 맞은 어린이들에게는 'How old are you?'라고 질문합니다. 케이크에 양초를 꽂고 나면 생일을 맞은 학생('birthday-girl' 혹은 'birthday-boy')이 불을 끄기에 앞서 소원을 빌도록 유도합니다. 불을 한 번에 끄게 되면 소원이 이루어진다고 생각하기도 합니다.

- Merry Christmas!
- Happy New Year/Chuseok/Easter/Independence Day!

- Enjoy the holiday!
- Have a good Chuseok!
- I hope you enjoy your Chuseok!

- What are your plans for the break?
- Are you doing anything special?
- What do you want to do this summer?
- What are you going to do on New Year's Eve/Day?
- How do you usually celebrate New Year's?
- Are you going to ...?

◦ We're going to do a service project.
◦ I hope to visit Hawaii next summer.
◦ I'm planning to take a math course.

- See you again after the break.
- We'll have class again on Monday.
- I guess I won't see you until after the holiday.

8 Saying Goodbye
작별 인사하기

Teacher: This is our last time together. You've been a good class. I'll miss you. I wish you all the best. Keep practicing your English.

- Good-bye.
- Bye-bye.
- So long.
- See you (around/later/tomorrow/on Monday).
- See you later.
- Take care.
- Take it easy.

도움말

다음 표현들의 차이에 주목할 필요가 있습니다.
    awkward: *See you again.
    correct: See you later.

- Have a good day.
- Have a nice day.
- Enjoy the weekend.
- Have fun this weekend.

(마지막 수업에서)

- This is our last time together.
- I won't see some of you anymore.
- I probably won't be working with you again next semester.

- I'll miss you.
- I enjoyed working with you.
- You've been a good class.
- I've had fun with you this semester.

- Keep practicing English.
- May your English get better and better.
- I hope you all get a chance to show off your English.

- Good luck!
- All the best!
- I wish you well.

- I wish you all the best.
- I know you will all succeed.
- I hope every one of you does great things in the future.

Appendix 1

Review Exercises and Answer Key

Appendix 1

Review Exercises and Answer Key
복습 문제 및 정답

Part 1   Review Exercises ··· 337
Part 2   Review Exercises ··· 341
Part 3   Review Exercises ··· 345
Part 4   Review Exercises ··· 348
Part 5   Review Exercises ··· 350
Part 6   Review Exercises ··· 352
Answer Key to Part 1 Review Exercises ················· 354
Answer Key to Part 2 Review Exercises ················· 357
Answer Key to Part 3 Review Exercises ················· 360
Answer Key to Part 4 Review Exercises ················· 362
Answer Key to Part 5 Review Exercises ················· 364
Answer Key to Part 6 Review Exercises ················· 366

Part 1 Review Exercises

I. Matching: Match the expression to the context.

Expressions:
1. 'Take one and pass them on.'
2. 'This is the material we covered while you were gone.'
3. 'Is there anyone who's name I didn't call?'
4. 'Let's give a warm welcome to Mr. Jeong.'
5. 'Welcome back.'
6. 'Bless you.'
7. 'Are there any extras?'
8. 'Is anyone absent?'
9. 'Just kidding.'
10. 'Remember this?'

Contexts:
A. You want the students to acknowledge that they have done this before.
B. A teacher greets a student who has been sick for several days.
C. The teacher wants the students to clap before a guest speaks.
D. Someone sneezed.
E. The class should distribute a handout among themselves.
F. The teacher wants to collect the leftover handouts after the handouts have been distributed.
G. The teacher is taking attendance, but the teacher will not read the class list.

Appendix 1 | 337

H. The teacher has just taken attendance by reading the class list. There may be some students in the room who are not on the list.

I. The teacher wants to explain that he just told a joke.

J. A student did not come to the last class. The teacher shows the student what the rest of the class did the previous day.

II. What would you say in the following situations:

1. You are going to introduce yourself to the students.
2. You want to tell students where to find you outside of class.
3. A new student has joined the class.
4. All of the students should use English names.
5. You want the students to respond in a certain way when you call the role.
6. You want to encourage a late student to come on time.
7. A student was sick last week. You want to ask about her health now
8. You want to make small talk by asking about what the students did over the weekend.
9. You want the students to describe the weather.
10. You want the students to express an opinion about the temperature of the classroom.
11. You want the students to turn their pagers and cell phones off during class.
12. In today's class, you will continue what were doing last time.
13. You want the students to make a space between the rows of desks.
14. You want the students to take out their English books.

15. You want to know if each student has a copy of the material that was distributed.

III. Here are the teacher's thoughts. Write what the teacher says.

1. That student didn't respond when I called his name because he wasn't listening.
2. I wonder where Hye-su is.
3. I'm very surprised.
4. I wish the air-conditioner were off.
5. I'd like some help.
6. I want the students to give me their homework.
7. I want the students to tell me what they remember from last class.
8. We should start the class.
9. I wonder who this pencil belongs to.
10. I'd like Jeong-mi to distribute the papers.

IV. Choose the right question. (The response is given.)

1. a) What day is it today?
   b) What's the date?
   response: It's Monday.

2. a) Do you have the time?
   b) Do you have time?

response: It's 3:20.

3. a) Who can share a pencil with Chong beom?
   b) Who has an extra pencil?
   response: I do.

4. a) Who's out in the hallway?
   b) Please ask Min-ho to come in.
   response: Min-ho is.

5. a) Is there anyone who didn't hear their name?
   b) Is anyone absent?
   response: Mi-sun is gone.

V. Circle the right word or words.

1. Do you have any other question/questions for me?
2. Did you wake up late this/today morning?
3. Do/Did you catch a cold?
4. Chul-hee was absent/absented.
5. That was a/my joke.
6. Is it okay if I let the blind/blinds down?
7. Straighten/Let's straighten your desks.
8. Let's put four chairs together in each group/groups.
9. I prepared/brought some pictures for you.
10. Is there anyone who doesn't have/receive a copy?

Part 2 Review Exercises

I. Here are the teacher's thoughts. Write what the teacher says.

1. We had better start this activity again.
2. We should start the break now.
3. I need to split the class into two groups.
4. These three students should work together.
5. Oh no. No one's volunteering for this activity.
6. I need to walk past this person.
7. I need to leave the classroom to talk to someone in the hallway for a minute.
8. I wonder if everyone understands this.
9. Maybe I should give them a hint to help them find the answer.
10. The students are all way too noisy.

II. What would you say to the following students? Give two examples.

Example: Sang-myeong was absent last class. He is here today.
Possible answers: Welcome back, Sang-myeong./Sang-myeong, we missed you yesterday.

1. The answer was 'butterfly,' but Sun-hee said '나비'.
2. Hyun-il is not joining in the choral repetition.
3. It was Oh-hoon's turn to answer, and Mi-sun whispered the answer to him.
4. You want Yeong-hee to begin a chain activity.
5. The students should be working in groups, but Min-jun is working alone.
6. Gil-sun said something, but you could not hear him.
7. Mi-ok answered a simple question correctly.
8. Mi-ok answered a very difficult question perfectly.
9. Min-cheol go the answer wrong, but you want to encourage him to try again.
10. Seung-hun is stressed out about an exam.
11. Won-ho didn't do his work very well.
12. Hyeok-gyu is playing carelessly with some expensive audio equipment.
13. Dong-myung is looking at something in the back of the room.
14. Gyung-hwa fell on the pavement.
15. Gi-dae offered to carry something for you.
16. You want Gwang-min to take a cookie from a tray.
17. You are handing a paper to Do-hyeon.
18. Mun-baek told you that he first prize in an essay competition.
19. Do-il said that his mother is very sick.
20. Byung-jeon lost a game.

III. Is the teacher talking to one student, two students, or the whole class?

1. Bo-ra, would you start?
2. We'll start with Bo-ra.
3. Everybody work individually.
4. Do you have a partner?
5. Let's divide into three groups.
6. Which team do you want to be on?
7. Who wants to do this?
8. Hee-jin is going to model this for us.
9. Stand by your chair.
10. Take your seats.
11. Nobody move.
12. Any questions?
13. Do you have a question?
14. If you have any questions, raise your hand.
15. Does that answer your question?
16. Do we all agree?
17. Can you tell me why you said so?
18. Let's take a vote.
19. Help yourself.
20. You may each have one.

IV. Choose the better word or words in each sentence.

1. Everyone speak./say, 'How's the weather?'
2. Let's take/change turns.
3. Make/Find a partner.
4. You can be on/in this team, okay?
5. Any volunteer/volunteers?
6. Follow my instruction/instructions.
7. Do how/what I say
8. Raise/Lift your hand.
9. Do/Are you understand?
10. I'll try to explain it/about it another way.
11. Do you want a/some help?
12. You can doit/well.
13. Try a little harder/hardly.
14. The movie was kind of bored/boring.
15. Don't cheat/cheating.

Part 3 Review Exercises

I. Tell students to correct the following mistakes.

example: 's-c-h-o-l'
correction: You need another 'o'./You have to have one more 'o'./It's spelled with two 'o's./Double 'o'.

1. 'N-E-E' (instead of 'K-N-E-E')
2. 'V-I-C-Y-C-L-E' (instead of 'B-I-C-Y-C-L-E')
3. 'dis' (instead of 'this')
4. 'a beauty garden' (instead of 'a beautiful garden')
5. 'She ate an apples'.
6. 'Yesterday morning I go to the store.'
7. 'She thought her future' (instead of 'She thought about her future.'
8. 'jumping around the corner from the store.'
9. 'l' (instead of 't' and 'i')
10. 'HappY' (instead of 'happy')

II. Matching: Match the expression to the situation.

1. Read my lips. What am I saying?
2. What else could you say?
3. What's this?
4. Pass it around the room.

Appendix 1 | 345

5. Can you guess what the story is about?
6. Take out a pen or pencil.
7. What's missing?
8. It was very close.
9. Do you know it by heart?
10. Do the motions.

A. The class is looking at an illustration for a reading activity.
B. The students should prepare to write something.
C. The students should each hold an object and look at it.
D. The teacher is going to say something silently.
E. The students should move as they sing a song.
F. The teacher removed one object from a tray while the students had their eyes closed.
G. The teacher wants to encourage the team that just lost the game.
H. The teacher is showing an object to the students. The students should identify it.
I. The students should try to sing something for memory— without looking at the words.
J. The students are brainstorming things they could say in a certain situation.

III. Choose the correct word or words in each sentence.

1. You need more stress on/at the second syllable.
2. Listen and repeat the tape/after the tape.
3. I'd like to introduce some new vocabulary/vocabularies.

4. Are there any word/words that are unfamiliar?
5. Who knows what this is/is this.
6. This means/meaning is 'very expensive'.
7. I this sentence correct/correct sentence?
8. I'm going to play it two/twice times.
9. What did/were they talking about?
10. Could you speak/say more clearly?
11. We are going to do a/some brainstorming.
12. Let's act/act out this dialogue.
13. I will grade you in/on how well you follow the rules.
14. Read loudly/out loud.
15. Let's sing/sing a song 'Ten Little Indians'.

Part 4 Review Exercises

I. What could you say if you want the students to do the following things.

1. The students should look at page 14. Their books are closed.
2. The students should be aware of the graph at the bottom of the page 13.
3. The students should take notes from the PPT.
4. The students should use the words on the cards a cue words for writing sentences.
5. The students should explain the difference between two pictures.
6. The students should share information to solve a puzzle in an information gap activity.
7. In a pre-reading activity, students should predict what an article is about.
8. After watching a finger puppet play, the students should make their own puppets.
9. After listening to the sound only of a video, students should predict what they will see when picture is added to the video.
10. The students should tell you if their headsets are not working.

II. Fill in the blank with the appropriate preposition.

1. Turn___ page 35.
2. What page is chapter five ___?
3. Look___ the bottom of the page.
4. What's the difference ___ the words in column A and column C?
5. Look___ the beginning of the second paragraph.
6. Can you find the second line ___ the bottom?
7. The index is ___ the back.
8. Use the word ___ the card as a cue.
9. Point ___ the card when you hear the word.
10. The answer is ___ the back (of the card.)
11. Put these ___ order.
12. What is this a picture ___?
13. Look at the instructions ___ your card.
14. Put one letter ___ each blank.
15. Write your own answers ___ the first column.
16. Tell your teammates ___ the paragraph you read.
17. Do you usually start ___ the back or the front when you read the newspaper?
18. Look for the advertisements ___ the first page.
19. First look ___ the headline.
20. Choose the best title ___ the article.
21. Oops. We're ___ the wrong place.
22. Put the puppets ___ your fingers.
23. Take the puppets ___.
24. I'll play it ___ you one time.
25. Put the USB stick ___ the USB drive.

Part 5　Review Exercises

I. What would you say in the following situations:

1. You want the students to explain what they learned in class today.
2. You want the students to assess how well they understood today's material. (You worked on language used in a restaurant.)
3. You want to the students to feel proud of their work in class.
4. You want the students to start preparing for the next test.
5. You want to warn the students that there is not much more time allowed for the test.
6. You are giving tests back to the students. The tests were handed in earlier.
7. You want the students to grade each other's papers.
8. You want the students to calculate their own score on a quiz.
9. You are assigning homework and you want people to do the assignments in groups.
10. You want the students to choose their own homework assignment.

II. Matching: Match the beginning of the sentence with the end.

1. Let's review what we
2. We'll come back to it
3. I hope you had as much fun
4. Your English is getting better
5. Capitalization will be
6. Are you ready
7. If you're finished, check over
8. Are there any
9. This assignment is worth
10. You don't have any

A. as I did.
B. on the test.
C. other answers?
D. homework.
E. did today.
F. ten points.
G. tomorrow.
H. your work.
I. for the test?
J. and better.

Part 6 Review Exercises

I. What would you say in the following situations?

1. You have a little bit of extra time before the end of class so you want to sing a song.
2. The students should stop working.
3. You are going to make some announcements.
4. You want to tell the students about a field trip you are taking tomorrow.
5. You want I-hoon to collect the picture cards that students have been using.
6. You want the students to clean the room.
7. The room is not completely clean yet.
8. Class is over and the students may leave.
9. You want to make small talk about what the students will do over vacation.
10. It the last moment of the last class. You want to make a positive final statement to the students.

II. Circle the correct word or words in each sentence.

1. We're almost/mostly out of time.
2. It's time to/for stop already.
3. I'd like a/the card back.
4. Does anyone still have/has a card?
5. Don't leave a/any pens, pencil cases, notebooks ...
6. Throw all of a/the trash away.
7. There's still something that need/needs to be put away.
8. I hope you enjoy a/your Chuseok.
9. Enjoy a/the weekend.
10. I hope everyone of you do/does great things in the future.

III. Is it countable, uncountable, or always plural?

1. vocabulary
2. glue
3. glue stick
4. scissors
5. practice as in 'We need some practice'.
6. help
7. pronunciation
8. blinds
9. homework
10. pairwork

Answer Key to Part 1 Review Exercises

I.

1-E, 2-J, 3-H, 4-C, 5-B, 6-D, 7-F, 8-G, 9-I, 10-A

II. (Possible answers):

1. Let me introduce myself./Let me introduce myself to you./Let's start off with introductions./I'd like to share a few things about myself.
2. If you want to meet me, you can come to the teacher's office./If you need to talk to me outside of class, you can find me in the teacher's office./When I'm not teaching, I'm usually at the teacher's office.
3. This is your new classmate, Min-ho. I'd like you to meet Min-ho./I'd like to introduce a new friend to you.
4. You'll use an English name in this class./I'd like you all to choose English names in this class./Could each of you make an English name for this class?
5. When I say your name, please say, 'Here'./When you hear your name, say, 'Here'./When I call your name, please respond by saying, 'Yes'.
6. Don't be late again./Try not to be late again./Try to be on time tomorrow./You should come to class by nine o'clock. For next time, remember: class starts at nine o'clock./You should really be here at the beginning of class.
7. How do you feel now?/How are you feeling today?/Are you feeling better now?/Are you getting over it?

8. Did you have a good weekend?/Did you enjoy the weekend?/Did you have a nice weekend?/Did you do anything interesting over the weekend?

III. (Possible answers):

1. You should pay attention./You should have been listening./Pay attention next time when I take roll.
2. Where's Hye-su?/Does anyone know where Min-ju is?/Did anyone talk to Han-jun today?/Does anyone know why Hyun-sook is gone?
3. You're kidding!/That's incredible!/I just can't believe that!/No way! Really?/Oh my goodness!/What a surprise!
4. We don't need the air-conditioner./I think we would feel better without the air-conditioner./It's too cold in here with the air-conditioner on.
5. Would you do me a favor?/Help me, please./Could you give me a hand?/Would you mind helping us out?/Chanhee, I have a job for you.
6. I'd like to collect he homework now./Could you hand your papers to the front?/Please send your assignments to your right./Please han-in your homework before you leave./Please give your homework to me on your way out./Don't forget to give me your homework before you go.
7. What did we do last time?/What do you remember about ...?/Do you remember what we talked about last time?/What words did we learn last time?
8. Shall we get started./Shall we begin?/Are you ready?/Let's get started./I think we can get started./It looks like we're ready to begin./Let's get down to work.

9. Who lost a pencil?/Did anyone lose a pencil?/Is anyone missing a pencil?/Whose pencil?/Whose pencil is this?/Does this pencil belong to anyone?/Is this your pencil?
10. Jeong-mi, would you hand these out?/Jeong-mi, would you pass these around?/Could you give a copy to everyone?

IV.

1-A, 2-A, 3-B, 4-A, 5-B

V.

1-questions, 2-this, 3-did, 4-was absent, 5-a, 6-blinds, 7-straighten, 8-group, 9-brought, 10-have

Answer Key to Part 2 Review Exercises

I. (Possible answers) :
1. Let's do it again./Would you mind starting over?/I think we better start over./Let's take it from the top./I want you to go back to the beginning.
2. Break time./Let's take a break./I'll give you a five minute break./Okay. You can relax for a few minutes.
3. Now, I'll divide you in half./First I'm going to split you down the middle./Let's split right down the middle./Get into two teams./Make two teams./Let me divide you into two teams.
4. Yeong-su, Jin yeong, and Myeong-ho, can you be a group?/Can the three of you make one group?/Why don't the three of you work together?
5. What! No volunteers?/Come on. I know one of you wants to volunteer./If no one volunteers, I'll have to pick someone.
6. Excuse me./Pardon me./Sorry, I need to get through./Could you let me through?
7. Excuse me for a moment./I'll be back in a minute./I'll be right back.
8. Do you understand?/Are you with me?/Are you following me?/Do you get it?/Do you know what I mean? Is that clear?/Does that make sense?/Is there anything you didn't understand?
9. Would you like a hint?/Do you want some help?/Here's a hint./I'll give you a clue.
10. Be quiet./Settle down./Calm down./Not so much noise please.

II. (Possible answers):

1. Right. Now how do you say that in English?/Exactly. Say the same thing. This time in English./Good. What do you call that in English?
2. You too, Hyun-il./You join in this time, Hyun-il.
3. Don't help him./It's Sunsik's turn./Don't give him the answer./Let him figure it out on his own.
4. Yeong-hee, would you start?/Yeong-hee, could you go first?/Yeong-hee, why don't you start us off?
5. Don't you have anyone to work with?/Don't you have a group?/Do you need someone to work with?
6. What?/Pardon?/Excuse me?/I'm sorry?/What was that?
7. Good./Yes./Right./Uh-huh.
8. Excellent!/Terrific!/Wonderful!/Fantastic!
9. Try again./Have another try./Okay. You can do it this time.
10. Don't worry./You'll do fine./I'm sure you'll do okay.
11. That wasn't very good./You can do better than that./Come on. Try a little harder.
12. No, don't./Don't do that./That's enough./Hey! Stop!/Stop it right now!
13. Face the front./Turn this way./Turn around and face me.
14. Are you okay?/Did you get hurt?/Does your leg hurt?
15. That's nice of you./Sure, thanks for offering. Oh would you? Thanks./That would be great./How nice of you.
16. Help yourself./Go ahead. Help yourself./Go ahead. Take one.
17. Here./Here you are./There you go.
18. Congratulations!/I'm glad to hear that!/Good for you!
19. That's too bad./Sorry to hear that./I'm sorry to hear the bad news.

20. Better luck next time.

III.

1-one student, 2-the whole class, 3-the whole class, 4-one student, 5-the whole class, 6-one student, 7-the whole class, 8-the whole class, 9-one student, 10-the whole class, 11-the whole class, 12-the whole class, 13-one student, 14-one student or the whole class, 15-one student, 16-the whole class, 17-one student, 18-the whole class, 19-one student, 20-the whole class

IV.

1-say, 2-take, 3-find, 4-on, 5-volunteers 6-instructions, 7-what, 8-raise, 9-do, 10-it, 11-some, 12-it, 13-harder, 14-boring, 15-cheat

Answer Key to Part 3 Review Exercises

I. (Possible answers):

1. What letter does it start with?/What's the first letter?/What letter comes first?/It starts with 'K'./The first letter is 'K'./What letter is missing?/What's the missing letter?/You need another letter at the beginning./What letter do you need here?
2. 'B' not 'V'./Make this a 'B'./Change this 'V' into a 'B'./This should be 'B' not 'V'./What letter does it start with?/What's the first letter?
3. Put your tongue between your teeth for the 'th'./When you say 'th,' you have to have your tongue between your teeth./Your tongue needs to be between your teeth when you say 'th'.
4. Can you make beauty into an adjective?/What's the adjective form of 'beauty'.
5. Singular or plural?/Should this be singular or plural?/Do you want singular or plural here?
6. What verb tense do we need here?/What kind of verb goes here?/Do we need present tense?/What tense do we need?
7. You need a preposition here./One word is missing./You're missing a word./What word is missing?/What preposition does 'think' take?/What preposition comes after 'think'?
8. This isn't a complete sentence./This doesn't have a subject./This is a fragment.
9. Cross your 't's and dot your 'i's.
10. The 'y' needs to sit on the line and it has a tail that hangs down./The tail goes below the line.

II.

1-D, 2-J, 3-H, 4-C, 5-A, 6-B, 7-F, 8-G, 9-I, 10-E

III.

1-on, 2-after the tape, 3-vocabulary, 4-words, 5-this is, 6-means, 7-sentence correct, 8-two, 9-were, 10-speak, 11-some, 12-act out, 13-on, 14-out loud, 15-sing

Answer Key to Part 4 Review Exercises

I. (Possible answers):

1. Open your books to page 14./Let's look at page 14./Please take out your books and turn to page 14.
2. On page 13, there's a graph./You can see a graph on page 13./You'll see the graph at the bottom.
3. You need to write this down./Copy this down in your notebooks./Please write down everything that's on the board.
4. Make a sentence using the word on the card./Fill in the blank with the word on the card./Use the word on the card as a cue./Use the word on the card to make a question.
5. How are these two pictures different?/Can you find the differences?/What's different between these two pictures?/What are the differences between these two pictures?
6. Work together./You have to help each other./You have to ask each other questions to figure out the answer./You need to share your answers to solve the puzzle./Use your partner's information to figure out the answer.
7. Can you guess what this article is about?/What do you think the article talks about?
8. Let's make our own finger puppets./Now it's your turn to make finger puppets./I want you all to make finger puppets like mine.
9. What do you think you will see in the video?/Where do you think the action will take place?/Can you guess what you will see when I show you the picture?

10. Can you all hear?/Does your headset work?/Can you hear with your earphones?/Are you having problems with your headphones?

II.

1-to, 2-on, 3-at, 4-between, 5-at, 6-from, 7-in, 8-on, 9-to, 10-on, 11-in, 12-of, 13-on, 14-in, 15-in, 16-about, 17-at, 18-on, 19-at, 20-for, 21-in, 22-on, 23-off, 24-for, 25-in

Answer Key to Part 5 Review Exercises

I. (Possible answers):
   1. Let's review what we did today./What did we do with ...?/Okay. so what did we talk about today?
   2. Did you get it?/Do you think you can order food in a restaurant?/Do you feel like you understood what we did today?
   3. You worked hard today./You did a good job today. I'm very happy with what we did./Thanks for concentrating so well today. I'm thoroughly impressed.
   4. We are going to have a test on this./You should start thinking about the test./We have an exam coming up.
   5. There are five minutes remaining./There are only five minutes left./You have five minutes.
   6. I'm going to return your tests now./Here are your tests./Would you come up here and get your test when I call your name?
   7. Trade papers with a friend./Give your paper to someone else./Could you exchange papers with someone sitting near you?
   8. Count up your points./Count how many points you got./Add up how many you got right.
   9. This is group work./You have to work with your group./Work together with your group.
   10. Choose one of the options to do as homework./You may do the assignment of your choice./Pick one of the options to do at home.

II.
1-E, 2-G, 3-A, 4-J, 5-B, 6-I, 7-H, 8-C, 9-F, 10-D

Answer Key to Part 6 Review Exercises

I. (Possible answers):

1. Let's end with a song. Let's sing one last song. Before you go, let's sing a little song./Last but not least, we'll sing 'She'll be Coming 'Round the Mountain'.
2. Okay. It's time to stop./That's all we have time for today./It looks like we have to stop now./Look at the time./We have to go./It's time to stop already. That went fast.
3. I have a few things to tell you./I have a couple of announcements to make./There are some important things for you to know.
4. We're going to go on a field trip tomorrow./Get ready for a field trip tomorrow./I have something special planned for tomorrow. We're going to go on a field trip.
5. I-hun, would you collect the cards for me? I-hun will come around and collect the cards. Give your cards to I-hoon. He's in charge of collecting them.
6. Let's clean up./We have a few minutes to straighten up./Please take a few minutes and put everything away.
7. There's still something on the floor./I see something that hasn't been put away yet./There's still something that needs to be put away.
8. It's time to go./You may go./You're dismissed.
9. What are your plans for the break? Are you doing anything special? What do you want to do this summer?
10. I wish you all the best./I know you will all succeed./I hope every one of you does great things in the future.

II.

1-almost, 2-to, 3-the, 4-have, 5-any, 6-the, 7-needs, 8-your, 9-the, 10-does

III.

1. uncountable 2. uncountable 3. countable 4. always plural
5. uncountable 6. uncountable 7. uncountable 8. always plural
9. uncountable 10. uncountable

Appendix 2

Making Classroom English Comprehensible

Appendix 2

Making Classroom English Comprehensible
교실영어 이해하기 쉽게 만들기

Making Classroom English Comprehensible
교실영어 이해하기 쉽게 만들기

by Heidi Nam
(2011, appeared in the KOTESOL Newsletter, *The English Connection*)

On paper, a policy of Teaching English In English (TEE) has a lot of benefits: it provides comprehensible input that is directly connected to the classroom environment and often requires a response from the students. In practice, however, many teachers find TEE difficult to implement in their own classes.

Teachers who are accustomed to teaching in the students' first language may find that the instructions that they normally use are not effective when translated directly into English. For example, a teacher might ask her third grade class, "들은 낱말을 누가 이야기해 볼까요?" and get a fine response, while a direct English translation like "Who will try saying the words they heard?" might elicit nothing but blank stares. Teachers will have much more success in English if they both pare down the number of concepts that they are trying to communicate and use more familiar vocabulary to communicate them. The resulting question might be something like, "What words did you hear?" The need to simplify concepts and perhaps even modify activities places an additional burden on teachers who switch the language of instruction to English.

It is often thought that native English speakers have an easier time simplifying their classroom English, but native English speakers have their own challenges to work through. Fluency itself enables them to overwhelm their students with too much input, spoken too fast. A rich vocabulary means that the first expression that comes to mind might not be one that a group of students would readily understand. Of course, when teachers learn more about the language and educational background of their students, they can increase their ability to guess which words and phrases will be most (or least) comprehensible to their students.

Regardless of the teachers' background, there are some tricks of the trade that can help teachers make their instructions more comprehensible to students. Quite often, the most effective explanation of an activity is a demonstration. For written exercises, the teacher can walk the students through the first exercise so that the students can see how they are supposed to respond to the input. Pair work activities could be demonstrated with co-teachers; otherwise, a teacher can demonstrate with a student, feeding the student the language necessary to get through the activity.

Simplifying the Message 메세지 단순화하기

When a verbal explanation is necessary, the teacher can simplify the message. In order to do this, the teacher needs to recognize the core message of the classroom instruction and weed out the unnecessary ideas. Sometimes teachers ramble. Ironically, when some teachers worry that their students might not be following their instructions, they explain more, which may end up overloading the students with input. There are several ways of keeping this tendency in check. The teacher could try writing out a teaching script, which could help the teacher think through which instructions are truly necessary. During class, if the teacher is unsure whether the students really got the message, she might try asking a specific question about the instructions rather than explaining them again.

In addition to cutting out extraneous words, the teacher can support comprehension by breaking the instructions into meaningful chunks. Since lists of oral instructions are easily forgotten, the teacher can help the students by focusing on what they need to do at the moment. Whenever there is an instruction that can be applied immediately, the teacher may stop and check that the students have successfully followed that chunk before going on to the next chunk. If the students need to understand a sequence of instructions, it may be better to write or project the instructions where they can be reread as necessary.

The teacher may also make ideas more comprehensible by making them more concrete. One way of doing this is using "I" and "you" language. Instead of using a third person prompt like "When it someone's birthday, what do people say to them?" she might use something like "It's my birthday. What do you say?" Another technique is to replace grammatical terminology with grammatical formulas. For example, instead of talking about "present progressive", the teacher can talk about "be + (verb)ing". Likewise, a teacher may want to replace functions with key expressions. Instead of saying, "We're going to learn how to talk about ability." the teacher may say, "We're going to learn can and can't."

Modifying delivery 전달 방법에 적절한 변화 주기

Once the message has been simplified, the teacher can also support student comprehension by changing the style of speaking. The following five delivery techniques (in ascending order from my least to most favorite) are often used to increase comprehension: the omission of function words, modification of pronunciation, slowness, repetition, and pauses.

The omission of function words (such as articles and prepositions) is a technique that many native English speakers use, resulting in short phrases akin to "Me Tarzan. You Jane." or "Get pencil." Although I have heard a number of teachers swear by the effectiveness of "Tarzan Talk,"

I suspect that the success may be attributable to clearer articulation or to the shorter phrases and the increased frequency of pauses. Since many learners frequently do not hear function words even when they are used, it seems unlikely that the omission of function words would increase these learners' comprehension.

Pronunciation can be modified in several ways to assist learners. Teachers might make their speech clearer by over-articulating consonants or by limiting their use of reductions (such as "gonna" for going to" and "dija" for "did you"). Some teachers also adopt features of Korean pronunciation in order to make their words more comprehensible to Korean learners. For example, they may add a vowel sound following /d/or /s/. Since these sounds are not articulated when they come at the end of a syllable in Korean, adding the extra vowel sound can make the final consonant more salient to some Korean listeners.

Although adding the extra vowel sound does aid comprehension for some learners, other learners don't need the help. Many of these learners have had a great deal of exposure to unmodified English, and they may find this kind of modified pronunciation patronizing. Furthermore, adopting features of Korean pronunciation can make the English less comprehensible to anyone who is not familiar with the style.

Pauses, repetition, and slowness all serve to reduce the number of words that the student needs to process in order to understand the teacher's instructions. Perhaps the most underused of these techniques is pausing. Sometimes teachers are afraid of silence, and so they avoid pauses. Yet pauses provide valuable time for listeners to take in what has just been said. If even native speakers are more likely to get a joke when the speaker pauses after the punch line, how much more do non-native speakers benefit from a moment to let the message sink in? Repetition is also useful because it reinforces an idea. Repetition should not, however, be used as a substitute for pausing; if the students don't seem to respond to the message immediately, they might need additional time to think. Like pausing and repetition, slowness can aid comprehension, but it provides neither processing time like pauses nor reinforcement like repetition.

Providing additional support 부가적인 지원 방법을 제공하기

Teachers can provide additional support when they introduce unfamiliar instructions. Translation or mime can help students get the instructions the first time, but the teacher has to be careful not to make the extra support a habit. When teachers make the extra support automatic, they may unintentionally train their students to watch the movement or wait for the translation rather than try to understand the instructions in English. To avoid this problem, after the students have heard the instruction a few times, the teacher can try giving the instruction without support. If the students can follow the instruction, then the extra support is no longer necessary.

How much should teachers simplify? 언어 단순화 시의 고려 사항

Teachers should be aware that there is a trade off when they simplify their language. Restricting vocabulary means that students have less varied input. While an elementary school student might appreciate that the teacher substitutes the key phrase "I'm sorry." for the function "apologize," a more advanced student may need the word "apologize" to discuss the formality of different ways of apologizing. Modifying delivery to make English more accessible to learners makes it less like the English used in conversations among native speakers. Slowness, over-articulation and the avoidance of reductions, for example, can all lead to separation of the words so that phrases lose common features of connected speech. Tarzan talk provides a model of English that would acceptable in few situations, and extra vowel sounds often lower comprehensibility outside of Korea.

Two factors should determine how teachers simplify their language. First, teachers should keep the learners' goals in mind. If the ultimate goal of the learner is to communicate in English as an International Language, then perhaps it is in the learner's best interest to learn a simple style of English that will be comprehensible to other non-native speakers. English with basic vocabulary and distinct pronunciation may be the most useful style for them to learn.

The second factor is the students' level. Obviously some groups of students need more assistance than others to understand the teacher talk. Finding the right amount of simplification for a particular group of students is a challenge in itself. Teachers need to regularly check whether their students understand. This could involve simply observing whether the students successfully follow the instructions. The teacher may also ask specific questions about the instructions ("How many sentences do you have to write?") or elicit an L1 translation ("How do you say that in Korean?") When simplification is well-targeted to the students' level, it will greatly increase the effectiveness of classroom English.

찾아보기

(ㄱ)

가산 명사 ·································· 100
감기 ·· 28
감사 ································· 161~162
개인 응답 ·································· 92
개인 활동 ·································· 99
게임 ···························· 175, 233~241
격려 ································· 133~134
격식 ·· 6
결석 ······························· 24~27, 77
경고 ································ 147, 152~154
경기 이름 ································ 234
과목/강의 소개 ··················· 73~77
관사 ······················· 39, 62, 171, 234
광고/광고자료 ················· 277~279
교과서 사용하기 ············· 253~259
교실 ······················ 3~4, 45~49, 67, 118
교재 수거 ································ 326
구두 언어 ································· 37
국가영어능력평가시험 ······ 313~314
규칙/규칙 설정 ········· 77, 147~149

그래프 ······························· 280~281
그룹 이름 ································ 105
그룹 활동 ······················· 103~107
그림 그리기 ····················· 247~249
그림카드 ··························· 268~270
글자 ·· 170
긍정문 ······································ 34
기자재 문제 ····················· 299~230

(ㄴ)

나누기 ······························· 163~164
날씨 ·· 42
날짜 ··································· 39~40
노래와 챈트 ····················· 242~246
노트 ·· 327
노트북 ···································· 327
녹화 ·· 290

(ㄷ)

다음 수업 준비 ······················ 324
단수 ······················ 66, 105, 108, 241

찾아보기 | 377

단어 ·················· 170, 175, 178,
　　181, 215, 257, 277, 289, 298, 307
단어카드 ························· 265~267
단어 목록 소개 ····················· 145
대답 ································ 55, 87
대명사 ································· 234
대화 ······························ 196~200
도움 ···································· 160
도표 ···························· 280, 281
동명사 ···················· 147, 158, 161
동사 ······ 26, 47, 66, 140, 242, 282
동의 ························· 55, 65, 139
동작 ······························· 112~117
동화 읽어주기 ························ 193
동화 제목 ····························· 193
듣기 ······························ 187~191

(ㄹ)
라임 배우기 활동 ···················· 234

(ㅁ)
말하기 활동 ···················· 313~314
명령어 ·································· 91
명사 ······················ 127, 138, 248
명사구 ··································· 39
명확성 ································· 194
모음 ··································· 171
목적어 ·································· 31
몸동작 ·································· 93
몸짓 언어 ······························ 37

무례한 표현 ·························· 129
문법 ··································· 182
문어 ··································· 145
미국영어 ································ 49

(ㅂ)
박수 ··································· 241
박자 ··································· 234
반복 ···················· 89, 130, 193
반응 ························· 37~38, 55
발음 ························ 4, 174~177
발표 ····························· 88, 111
백판 ······························ 260~264
번역 ···································· 87
벽 그림/벽 포스터 ··················· 276
보여주며 말하기 ············· 201~203
복수형 ·································· 13,
　　108, 113, 138, 170, 271, 294
복습 ············ 53~55, 104, 303~305
부가의문문 ····························· 55
부동의 ·································· 65
부사형 ·································· 14
부정사 ·································· 91
부정적인 표현 ······················· 129
부탁 ···································· 46
분반 ·································· 97~98
불가산 명사 ····················· 83, 100
브레인스토밍 ························ 195
비디오 녹화 자료 ············ 285~289
비밀 ·································· 235

빔(Beam) 프로젝터 ·········· 291~292

(ㅅ)

사과 ································· 158~159
사진 ································· 268~270
새로운 수업 내용으로 이동·· 56~57
색/색깔 ································· 248
생일 ····································· 330
선택형 질문 ····························· 12
선행사 ·································· 35
선호하는 것 ······················ 141~143
설명 및 예시 ······················ 144~145
설명 요청 ························· 123~124
성취감 ································· 130
소개 ································· 8~14
소리 크기 요청 ····················· 194
소원 ··································· 330
소유격 ·································· 62
소유대명사 ···························· 39
손가락 인형 ······················ 282~284
손님/새로 온 학생 소개 ······ 15~16
손으로 쓰기 ······················ 225~226
수업 내용 보충 ···················· 31~33
수업 내용의 순서 ················ 79~81
수업 다시 시작 ······················· 85
수업 자료 ·························· 60~68
수업 전 사소한 이야기 ······· 33~36
수업 종료 ············ 321~323, 329
수업 진도 ··························· 82~83
수업 통제 ···························· 146

숙제 ···················· 50~52, 315~318
순서 교체 ··························· 93~96
숫자 ····································· 81
스포츠 팀의 이름 ··················· 108
시간 ····································· 41
시험 ······························ 306~314
신문 ······························ 277~279
신체적인 반응 ························ 116
실례 ······································ 4
실수 ······························ 129~130
쓰기 ······························ 221~226

(ㅇ)

알파벳 ·························· 170~171
어학 실습실 ··················· 293~294
어휘 ······························ 178~181
억양 ···································· 130
여론 조사 ···························· 143
연극 ······························ 204~207
연습문제/연습활동 ·········· 227~232
영어사용 ··························· 86~87
영국영어 ······························· 49
영어 이름 ··························· 17~18
오늘의 수업 소개 ····················· 78
오디오 녹음 자료 ············ 285~289
요구 ·························· 91, 116
요약 ···································· 219
요청 ······················· 3~4, 45~46, 65
용기 ···································· 120
워크시트 ······················· 271~273

찾아보기 | 379

워크카드 ······················ 271~273
유도 ··································· 91, 116
융판 ·· 275
응답 ······················ 12, 37~38, 89~92
의견 제시 ···························· 137~140
이름 ······························ 17~18, 325
이야기 요약하기 ·························· 219
이야기 말하기 ······················ 192~193
이해력 점검 ························ 119~122
인사 ······························ 5~7, 330~333
일반 활동 ···························· 112~117
읽기 활동 ···························· 215~220

(ㅈ)

자기 수정 ··································· 130
자리 배치/자리 정리 ············· 58~59
자석판 ································ 260~264
자신감 ································ 110~111
자원 ···································· 110~111
자음 ··· 171
작별 인사 ···························· 332~333
재채기 ·· 29
전체 반복 ···································· 90
전치사 ······················· 9, 31, 91, 266
절기 인사 ···························· 330~331
정관사 ·· 95
정답 유도 ···························· 131~132
정리 ··································· 327~328
정보차 활동 ································ 274
정중하게 말하기 ················· 22, 170

제스처 ·· 59
제안/제시 ············· 18, 75, 91, 137~143
종료 시간 알리기 ················· 321~322
주어 ·· 66
주의 집중 ································· 150
지각 ··································· 21, 77
지도 ·································· 280~281
직접목적어 ································ 91,
  140, 190, 242, 282
질문 ······································· 120,
  130, 156, 169, 204, 305, 307, 330
질병 ·· 28
질의응답 ············· 37~38, 89~92, 307
집중 ··· 151
짝 활동 ······························ 100~102

(ㅊ)

챈트 ··································· 245~246
철자 ··· 181
철자법 ······································ 169
촌극 ··· 204
추론 ··· 235
추측 ··· 237
추측 게임 ················ 175, 235, 266
축하/축복 ························· 165~166
출석 ····································· 19~30
칠판 ·································· 260~264
칭찬 ································ 43~44, 120

힌트 주기 ·································· 181

(ㅋ)

카드 ································ 265~273
카드 게임 ···························· 266
컴퓨터 ······························ 295~298
퀴즈 ···································· 306
큰 소리로 읽기 ······················ 216

(ㅌ)

토론 ························· 208~214, 219
팀 나누기 ························ 108~109

(ㅍ)

페이지 ······························ 256~259
평가 ···················· 135~136, 306~314
피드백 제공 ··························· 125
필기 ······································ 327
PPT 기기 ··························· 291~292

(ㅎ)

학생 발표 ································· 88
한국어/영어 사용 ················ 86~87
핸드폰 ····································· 49
허락 ·································· 155~157
현재 시제 ······························· 219
형용사 ······························· 26, 248
호칭 ··· 4
확인 ············· 55, 87, 126~130, 169
활동 종료 ······························· 323
훈육 ································· 146~149
휴식 시간 ································ 84